The Romance

Novel Formula

How to Use the Complete Structure of True Love

for Your Breakout Romance Novel

By Alicia Leigh

Books by A.K. Leigh/Leigh Hatchmann/Alicia Leigh

The Smithfield Series – A.K. Leigh
(Romantic Suspense)
See Her Run
Crave Her Touch
Trust Her Heart

The Farris Triplets Series – A.K. Leigh
(Crime Romance)
Triple Threat
Triple Terror
Triple Trouble

The Easter in Hallston series – A.K. Leigh
(Contemporary Romance)
Easter Love Connection
Easter Love Match
Easter Love Reunion

The Bloodworth Family Series – Leigh Hatchmann
(Paranormal Romance)
Vengeance of the Witch
Curse of the Witch
Sister of the Witch
Brother of the Witch

Standalone Books – A.K. Leigh
To Catch A Christmas Thief *(Romantic Suspense)*
The Venus Cure *(Romantic Suspense)*
The Million Dollar Secret *(Contemporary Romance)*
Rescuing Dr. Burgess *(Contemporary Romance)*

Standalone Books – Leigh Hatchmann
A Time to Love *(Time Travel Romance)*
Beautiful *(Retelling of Beauty & The Beast)*

Collections and Anthologies – A.K. Leigh
A Little Bit of Love: Short Story Romance Collection
The Smithfield Series Collection

The Writer's Magic Series – Alicia Leigh (non-fiction)
The Dreaming Writer
The Romance Novel Formula

Find A.K. Leigh/Leigh Hatchmann/Alicia Leigh online

Website – www.fallinlovewithleigh.com
Bookbub – www.bookbub.com/authors/a-k-leigh
YouTube –
www.youtube.com/channel/UCskieRmAicWgBXo7Cg
U5McA
Facebook – www.facebook.com/AuthorAKLeigh
Instagram – www.instagram.com/akleighauthor
Amazon – www.amazon.com/author/akleigh and
www.amazon.com/author/leighhatchmann
* A.K. Leigh is not currently on Twitter*

The Romance Novel Formula: How to Use the Complete Structure of True Love for Your Breakout Romance Novel

The Romance Novel Formula
ISBN: 978-0-6453711-0-9
First published: 2021
Cover design by: Sarah Paige (Opium House Creatives)
Edited by: Belinda Holmes
Revision and proofing by: Alicia Leigh
Formatting by: Alicia Leigh

To report a typographical error, please visit
www.fallinlovewithleigh.com

Table of Contents

Act 4 checklist

How long should Act 5 be?
The purpose of Act 5
How do I start the fifth act?
How many beats make up the fifth act?
Beat 10—Come together
Examples of the tenth beat in romance novels
Beat 11—H.E.A. or H.F.N.
Examples of the final beat in romance novels
How do I end the fifth act?
Act 5 checklist

What now?
That's all, my "loveleigh" romance writers!

About Alicia Leigh

Alicia Leigh is a bestselling non-fiction author, international-selling romance author, identical triplet, writing coach, and hot chocolate addict.

She uses her postgraduate degrees in counseling from the Australian College of Applied Psychology and editing from Macquarie University to create believable, three-dimensional characters. Her certificates in forensic science and forensic anthropology from the University of Strathclyde add layers to the realistic crime elements in her stories. She has completed her master's degree in writing at Swinburne University and is currently embarking upon her PhD in Creative Arts (writing) at Central Queensland University.

When not writing, reading, coaching, studying, or enjoying nature, she can be found having fun with her three gorgeous children (plus one laid-back dog and three noisy guinea pigs).

She is active on social media and encourages readers and writers to interact with her there. She writes romantic fiction novels under the pseudonyms A.K. Leigh and Leigh Hatchmann.

You can become a "loveleigh" by visiting:
www.fallinlovewithleigh.com
Fall in love ... with Leigh

Introduction

Is there a formula in romance novels?

"There is no formula—only a format, as with all genre fiction, which allows room for creative expression, unique writing voices and memorable characters."

From the Mills & Boon website.

"Romance novels are written to a specific formula." The number of times I've heard this insulting and patronizing phrase throughout my career as a romance writer would fill its own book! Yet, regardless of urban legends and popular culture tales, the simple fact is this: There is no romance novel formula.

Let me repeat that with emphasis: *There is no romance novel formula.*

Now, it may seem I have contradicted the title of this book by saying that. However, there is more than one way to write a romance novel. This book is intended as a guide to assist you while giving you the freedom to find your own version of a formula.

While there is no set formula per se, there *is* a structure you can follow that will aid you in writing your breakout romance novel. This structure isn't used solely by romance writers. Different forms are used by all novelists (see, for instance, books such as *Story, Save The Cat! Writes a Novel, The Plot Whisperer*, and *Story Engineering,* which have a variety of formulas, guides and suggestions). In that regard, writing a romance novel is almost the same as writing any other novel. I say almost because the romance genre has necessary inclusions that are applicable to it alone. This applies to every genre. These are called *genre conventions.*

Whether you are a novice or a seasoned writer, this book can lead you through the quagmire of structure and help you find the unique path for your characters to follow on what I call *the lovers' journey.*

The definition of a romance novel

Before we begin, it seems pertinent to understand exactly what a romance novel is—and isn't. This is the working definition I used during my master's degree research, with a slight modification: a work of fiction that includes a love story as the central element, between two or more characters, with a happy and satisfying ending.

Sounds simple enough, right? Just remember that the H.E.A. (happily-ever-after) and "a love story as the central element" are absolute necessities for your story to fit in the romance category. The way you get there is up to you. Another point to keep in mind is that the H.E.A. can also be a H.F.N. (happy-for-now). This means you no longer have to end your story with a wedding—but you can if you want to!

As of publication, I am the author of over twenty romance and non-fiction books that have sold both at home (Australia) and around the world. My books have been published by Pan Macmillan and Harlequin Publishing, as well as through independent publishing.

My first non-fiction book, *The Dreaming Writer*, was a number one Amazon bestseller in the U.S.A. upon its release in 2019. Along with this, my novel, *Beautiful*, peaked at number thirteen on the Amazon America charts in 2020.

You can find out more about me and my writing at: www.fallinlovewithleigh.com

How is this book different?

The main research I carried out as part of my master's degree revolved around the structure of romance novels (specifically, any common beats they shared). During my research, I discovered that little had been done in the academic field on romance novels and their structure. Considering the popularity of, and my passion for, the romance genre, I found this to be disturbing. I wanted to add to the available knowledge to provide both academics and romance writers with more information.

Furthermore, though there are some fantastic books and blogs that list their own proposed structures of romance novels, the conclusions drawn are often *not* the result of academic research. *The Romance Novel Formula* is the culmination of thorough research and is presented to you in the hopes that your path to becoming a successful romance writer is made easier. This is not to say that the experiences of other romance writers (and the structures they have created) are not as relevant as the research I have undertaken, because they most certainly are. In fact, some of the tips I provide throughout are based on my own experiences. Even so, I feel that my merging of both academic knowledge and experience is another advantage of this book.

It will also guide you step-by-step in taking your novel from idea to first draft. That's right, if you follow the exercises in this book, you will have a complete first draft at the end. No more half-finished manuscripts!

Will examples be used throughout?

Yes. Three of the novels I analyzed during my master's degree research will be used to showcase examples of *The Romance Novel Formula* throughout. As you will see, the formula is applicable to both modern and classic romance novels.

For those of you who have not read the books, a brief synopsis is included, along with further explanations as needed. You are *not* required to read the books (though I do recommend them!). The three novels are:

- o *Beautiful* by Leigh Hatchmann (one of my fiction pseudonyms)

  A modern retelling of the beloved fairytale *Beauty and the Beast*. Kit is a science experiment gone wrong. Part-man, part-beast, he lives in a cave on the edges of a private community and hides from the world. Until the night he intervenes and saves Bella from an unprovoked attack. Though they come from different worlds, the more time they spend together, the more a magical bond begins to form between them. And when the haunted secrets of his past collide with the darkness of her present, they will both discover exactly what makes someone beautiful.

o *Pride and Prejudice* by Jane Austen

The classic "I hated him, but now I love him" story. Mr. Fitzwilliam Darcy is one of the most eligible bachelors in England. The problem? It seems he is too proud to associate with the middle class. That doesn't bother the spirited and intelligent Elizabeth Bennet. She laughs off his rudeness—and forms a prejudiced opinion of him that refuses to budge despite the increasing amount of time they spend together. But when a scandal almost ruins her family, Elizabeth realizes how much her prejudice has blinded her to the truth about Mr. Darcy ... and he understands the devastating effects of being too proud.

- *Boyfriend Material* by Alexis Hall

  Reckless and somewhat-famous Luc O'Donnell risks losing his job after another compromising photo of him appears online. He needs someone who is "boyfriend material" to help clean up his shabby public image. Enter the clean-cut and reliable barrister, Oliver Blackwood, who can see the benefits of pretending to date Luc. With each date, the boundaries between fake and real blur. After a family party highlights long-denied problems, Oliver learns it can be okay to not have everything together and Luc finds he might be boyfriend material after all.

I repeat that though it would be helpful to you to have read these books, it is not essential to your overall understanding of the concepts in this book as everything will be explained in greater detail as we go along.

Does *The Romance Novel Formula* work best for "plotters" or "pantsers?"

Both! If you are a plotter, you can use it to outline your novel. If you are a pantser, you can use it after you've finished your first draft to make sure you have everything where it needs to be. Of course, you can also do something in between those two options. The point is to find what works for you.

If you are new to writing, you might not have heard of these terms, so I will give you a quick explanation here. For those who already know, feel free to skip ahead.

A plotter is a writer who plans every stage of their writing. They plot and outline every important part of their story before they write it. James Patterson is a famous plotter. This approach can stop you from running into trouble as you write because you always have a clear direction to go. On the other hand, it can also stifle your creativity and make it difficult when a character goes off script (which happens).

A pantser is a writer who writes by the seat of their pants. In other words, they go wherever their ideas, the story, or the characters take them. Stephen King is a famous pantser. This method can be great for those who revel in the creative side of storytelling. However, with no clear plan, the ideas can dry up and manuscripts can go unfinished.

As you can see, there are benefits to both. Though some people will try to convince you one is better than the other, the fact that so many writers are successful using either method tells you they are equally valid options.

In case you are curious, I am a plantser (just what you want, another unfamiliar term!). This means I utilize aspects of both plotting and pantsing in my writing. You can feel free to do the same.

A quick note on some terms used in this book

Throughout this book, I use *love interest 1* and *love interest 2* rather than the traditional hero and heroine. That way *all* main characters—including those that are alien or beast, or those of different sexual orientation—are accounted for.

Love interest one is the main character (the one who usually starts the book) and love interest two is the second main character. If your story contains ménage, harem, or polyamorous elements, everything discussed as part of the love interest two scenario is equally relevant and applicable to your other love interests.

The term *the lovers' journey* refers to the path undertaken, alone as well as together, by the love interests, which leads them to their happy ending.

A quick note on the format of this book

My aim in writing *The Romance Novel Formula* was to cater to all writers wherever they were on their writing journey. As such, some of the information will seem basic to established writers.

For instance, I have included chapters on essential writing skills. Some of these are relevant to general fiction writing (such as setting, theme, and dialogue), whereas others are romance specific (like the "meet cute"). If you feel you have a handle on these already, you can skim or skip those parts.

I also detail the romance arcs, acts and beats that make up the heart of *The Romance Novel Formula*. Though established writers will be familiar with these terms, the meanings and structure *will* be different to those listed in other books. Remember, this is based on the research I undertook which was aimed directly at the romance genre. For beginners who are unfamiliar with the terms, it will be explained at the appropriate place, so don't fret.

In using this book, I'd like to paraphrase the marvelous Bruce Lee, "Take what is helpful, discard what isn't, and add what is uniquely your own."

Are you ready to take your first step on the lovers' journey?

Chapter One

Preliminaries

The first step on the lovers' journey starts where every other journey starts: the beginning. There are several essential and fundamental writing skills that every successful author employs in crafting their novels. Some are romance specific, but most are relevant to every genre.

These are the preliminary skills you will need to develop. They will make your romance novel compelling and give it depth. Where structure (discussed in chapter two) can be thought of as the trees—the individual elements needed to comprise the whole—everything in this chapter can be thought of as the forest—the bigger picture parts you need to bring the smaller elements into focus.

As you move through the explanation of each skill set, you will find an accompanying exercise for you to complete. The answers you provide to these exercises can be transferred to the worksheet in Appendix A and used as the first part of an outline for your novel. Yes, that means you can finish an entire section of your novel outline by the end of this chapter. How exciting is that!

Let's step into the forest with the one thing I am sure you are craving to know.

What romance readers want from their fiction

When readers pick up a book, there are conscious and subconscious reader wants at play in the decision. These wants form the reasons one book is chosen over another. According to the Romance Writers of America website, there are three main reasons people read romantic fiction. These are:

- o Entertainment
- o Escape
- o Relaxation.

Is there a way you can include at least one (three is better) of these reader wants into your story? How will you do this? Is it unique enough to stand out? How can you expand on the terms? For instance, what does the word "entertainment" conjure up for you? There are many ways to be entertained. Is it comedic, mind-bending, enthralling, or heart-pumping? Jot down your answers to these questions, along with the reader wants you could target with your book, in the space provided below. You can also transfer your response to the worksheet at the back of the book (Appendix A), or you might prefer to make notes on a pad.

Exercise 1. What romance readers want from their fiction
Which *reader wants* does your manuscript offer? Circle those that might apply:

Entertainment   Escape   Relaxation

Further notes_____

_____

_____

Theme

Successful authors of all genres include at least one theme in their books that expresses and encircles their ideas about life and human nature. The romance genre is no different. To make your book stand out, it should contain a main overriding theme, something the reader can identify or empathize with. It can be a question the author poses to the reader, or it can be an existential truth, moral, or universal lesson.

Sometimes you will be conscious of this theme from the beginning of your writing, other times it will emerge as you write. Either way is fine. If your theme is not immediately apparent, don't freak out; you can come back to it once the final draft is complete and you see the story and your intentions in its entirety.

For instance, in my novel *Beautiful*, the main theme is "what is beauty?" In *Pride and Prejudice*, it could be "what is pride and what is prejudice?" (along with several others). In *Boyfriend Material* it is "first impressions can be false."

Twelve of the most common themes are:

- o Good always overcomes evil

- Anyone can triumph over suffering so long as you remain resilient
- Love will win in the end
- Family is everything
- True friendship means acceptance
- Home is where the heart is
- It is not wise to take the easy path
- Everybody is somebody
- War is a pointless tragedy
- Justice is not always just (and revenge can be bittersweet)
- Nobody can escape their past
- Growing up sucks.

Do any of the above spark familiarity? Can you name any books with one of these themes? How did you know that was the theme? Keep in mind that themes are rarely stated directly. Readers must often infer this information through metaphors, dialogue, characters, description, plotlines, locations, settings, motifs, and symbols. Have a look at some of these aspects to your novel. Is there a common theme you can spot and draw out a bit more?

Ponder the possible main theme that could come out of your manuscript then pop it into the section below—or your notebook and Appendix A.

Exercise 2. Main theme

What main theme could express your ideas about life and/or human nature?

_____

_____

_____

Further notes_____

_____

_____

Tone, Mood, Atmosphere

These three concepts fall under the category of advanced writing skills and, as such, can be confusing. I'll try to keep it as simple as possible (but don't worry if it takes you a while to catch the nuances!).

Though your story needs to contain all three of these elements, it is important to note that they don't necessarily need to be given the same level of importance. To prove this for yourself, as each part is explained, have a think about your favorite books and how these aspects show up in them.

Firstly, the author's particular *approach* to a character or situation in the story is the *tone*. Do you give your characters a bright, optimistic perspective, or is it secretive and dark? Something in the middle? A mixture? How do you distinguish your characters and situations in a way that makes them unique? What word choices have you made? Does this add to the tone you want to achieve, or does it detract from it?

The tone helps to set the *mood* of the story, which is the *feeling* (or feelings) generated in the reader. Does your story, and its scenes, leave the reader feeling happy, hopeful, sad, poignant, lighthearted, amused, scared? That is your mood. In romance fiction, you obviously want a romantic mood, but this can be supplemented with secondary and tertiary moods (for instance, suspense).

Atmosphere can be a tricky concept to define, and even harder to achieve with success. It is created by a mixture of both the mood and tone and allows the reader to *experience* the story as if they are immersed in it. It is sometimes referred to as the *reader experience*. Have you ever felt like you were inside a story, or lost in a book? This is atmosphere.

To summarize:

- o Tone is the author's individual *approach* to the characters or situation (how they describe the character or situation. It also encompasses word choices and style)
- o Mood is the *feeling* this approach gives the reader (happy, sad, terrified, for example)

o Atmosphere is the overall *experience* this gives the reader (is it a romantic experience, a thrill ride, a sense of mystery?).

What could your tone, mood, and atmosphere be? Do you feel one would make your story stronger than the others? Which one? Write your notes in the space below and transfer to your notebook or Appendix A.

Exercise 3. Tone/Mood/Atmosphere
List some ways you add a unique *tone* (approach) to your work:

_____

_____

_____

_____

_____

What overall *mood* (feelings) are you looking to convey?

_____

_____

_____

_____

_____

What *atmosphere* (reader experience) are you hoping to create for the reader?

_____

_____

_____

_____

_____

Time, Setting, Place

In order to imagine your story to life, readers need physical items and locations to lock onto—unless you are purposely going for a disjointed or ungrounded mood, but this is an advanced writing technique best left to well-versed writers.

The rest of us need to ground our readers in setting, place, and time.

Setting and place are closely linked. Where is your story set (what country, state, suburban, rural or city area), and at what place do the pivotal actions happen (a house, bedroom, car)?

Time refers not only to the position of the hands on a clock, but also to the year, month, and day of the week. Is your story set in modern times or the 1800s? Earlier? The future? Is your scene happening at midnight or noon? If you don't know this, how can your reader?

Note these in the exercise section below, and remember to include the season and weather as well.

Exercise 4. Time/Setting/Place
What setting, year, season, weather, places, and times do you need to keep track of in your novel?

_____

_____

_____

_____

_____

_____

Plot devices and tropes

A plot device is an object, event, image, theme, or character whose primary purpose is to drive the plot forward, create reader interest, investment, familiarity, and connection, maintain the story flow, and/or resolve or cause conflicts. Tropes are common plot devices used in storytelling. They have, arguably, been used by writers for centuries. As such, readers are familiar and comfortable with them which is why they are used to create instant connection and investment.

They are most often associated with the romance genre—usually as justification to denigrate it—but *all* genres employ them. For instance, horror and gothic novels have the haunted house and crime stories lead with the hardened detective. In the romance genre, some of the more familiar tropes include the love triangle, the beast, and the naive virgin.

Even though tropes can include well-known character types (like the beast), they are not to be confused with stereotypes and archetypes. Stereotypes are usually insulting caricatures, such as when women are given two options: the whore or the virgin mother. Archetypes are symbolic representations (more on this soon).

Most romance novel readers are familiar with tropes, whether consciously or sub-consciously, so you need to know what you are doing when you use them (and you *should* use them). A thorough list of some of the most common tropes used in the romance genre can be found under the following exercise. Keep in mind that everything you have written in your exercise sections or on your worksheet can be refined as you work on your novel—and that applies to your tropes as well.

On a final note, there is something I call a *writerly trope*. This is an idea, phrase, character, or image that is repeatedly used in a writer's work. Think about Jane Austen and her use of middle-class women as heroines. This is one of her writerly tropes.

I tend to have trust as an overarching idea in my novels. Hence, this could be classed as my writerly trope. Have a think about your writerly trope then add this to the appropriate exercise section, and in your notebook or preliminaries worksheet.

Exercise 5. Tropes

Visit www.fallinlovewithleigh.com/writingtips for a list of
the ninety most common romance tropes. Peruse the list
then note 1–3 that would suit your novel in the space
provided below.

_____

_____

_____

_____

_____

Do you have a writerly trope? Write it here:

_____

_____

_____

Master plots

Plot is the outline of events in a story. Even more
simplistically, it is what happens in the beginning, middle,
and end. As an aside, *story* refers to the specific events that
occur in your novel, while *narrative* is the way that you tell
the story. I know the differences between plot, story, and
narrative seem subtle, but the more you write, the easier it

will be to understand. For the purposes of this section, you only need to focus on your plot—the sequence of events in your story.

Some researchers and theorists, such as R. Porter Abbott (*The Cambridge Introduction to Narrative*) and Ronald Tobias (*20 Master Plots: and How to Build Them*), have concluded there are common master plots. These are plots readers find most appealing due to collective cultural identity. Abbott and Tobias have shown that the closer a story is to a master plot, the more credibility is assigned to it.

The twenty master plots according to Ronald Tobias are available on my website at www.fallinlovewithleigh.com/writingtips, along with my brief explanation of them. Look over the master plots, then write any you think would be relevant to your story in the exercise below.

Exercise 6. Relevant master plots

What is at least one relevant master plot for your novel?

_____

_____

_____

_____

_____

Archetypes

Carl Gustav Jung said archetypes are a "primitive mental image inherited from the earliest human ancestors and supposed to be present in the collective unconscious." How does this relate to writing and storytelling?

In the context of writing characters, archetypes are the character types that are widely recognized in popular culture. Stories that employ archetypal characters tend to do much better commercially than those that don't. Hence, you want to include archetypes in your writing.

How do you do that?

Firstly, you avoid stereotypes. Remember what I said about them a moment ago? I will repeat it here:

stereotypes are usually one-dimensional *insulting caricatures* whereas archetypes are *symbolic representations* that speak to the collective unconscious of humanity. Archetypes stir something primal inside of us and, therefore, make us bond with them. Stereotypes make us recoil or, at a minimum, give us a negative impression that impedes bonding.

By focusing on archetypes, you can create well-rounded, three-dimensional characters readers will feel connected to. Therefore, use one archetype for each of your main love interests. If you choose one for all your other main characters—including your antagonist—it will make your work stronger.

Please feel free to delve into this topic further as what I'm providing is a starting point only. There are many views when it comes to archetypes, including what I consider to be relevant cultural, colonial, and feminist perspectives. Not all of these stances are positive. Even so, when it comes to writing, I have found that including some sort of archetype boosts the story.

For more information, you might wish to check out *Feminist Archetypal Theory* by Estella Lauter and Carol Schreier Rupprecht, Joseph Campbell's *Hero with a Thousand Faces*, Carl Gustav Jung's *The Archetypes and The Collective Unconscious*, and *Women Who Run with the Wolves* by Clarissa Pinkola Estés.

An overview of twelve commonly accepted archetypes is available on my website at www.fallinlovewithleigh.com/writingtips. As you read through each of the archetypes, think of how they could show up in your own writing. Read through the archetypes, decide which are most applicable to your characters, then complete the following exercise.

Exercise 7. Archetypes
Which archetypes suit your main love interests?

_____

_____

_____

Where's the bond?

Remember, you are writing romance. As such, there needs to be a deep level of bonding that occurs between the main characters … and readers need to be able to feel this for themselves. Don't TELL them what they are feeling. If there is one area where you must show and not tell, bonding is it.

I think there are five levels of bonding necessary to create a realistic bond between your love interests (but feel free to experiment with this for yourself!). These are: physical, emotional, mental, sexual, and spiritual.

Physical is obvious. It is the attraction your characters experience when they see each other. It can incorporate everything on the spectrum from immediate lust to innocent appreciation. However, this is not enough to sustain a relationship—in either the real or book world. You can find someone physically attractive and not want to sleep with them or create a life with them, right? The same applies to your characters. There needs to be more than a physical bond.

This is where the emotions come in. An emotional connection is established between the characters when they are able to be vulnerable with each other. Show them sharing their thoughts and feelings, and inviting the other love interest/s into their inner world.

Next comes the mental bond. Emotional and physical bonding is fantastic, but having a topic, or two, that you can talk about in between all that lust and emotion helps gel the relationship and move the emotional connection forward. It also helps in the *getting to know you* stage (more on this in the beats section in chapter three). For now, think about what common interests the characters could share.

The sexual bond can be confused with the physical, but again, just because you find someone physically attractive, it does not automatically translate into sexual interest. Think of the times you met someone and found them physically attractive but had no urge to sleep with them. Sexual connection is a separate category. As such, make sure you show these bonds as two different elements to really drive the belief in the romance to the reader. Sexual trust, intimacy, and compatibility also comes into this and needs to be shown (not told!).

I am sure you are asking by now: What is a spiritual bond? It is *not* related specifically to religion or tantra (though it can). The spiritual bond is the "higher level" the characters feel they have reached by being with the other/s. It incorporates sharing things not shared before—the so-called "good" and "bad" parts of ourselves and secrets from our pasts—and being accepted for it. The growth the characters go through, which impacts the relationship in a positive way, can also be included in the spiritual bond. As can the feeling that the relationship is fated or destined, but don't go overboard with this one or it can be seen as cheesy and clichéd.

How much bonding do your characters experience in your story? Could you add more? Write your answers below, and on your worksheet or in notebook.

Exercise 8. How can you show the five romantic relationship bonds in your story?

Physical_____

_____

_____

_____

Emotional_____

_____

_____

_____

Mental_____

_____

_____

_____

Sexual_____

_____

_____

Spiritual_____

_____

_____

_____

_____

The five characters every novel should have

Regardless of genre, you will find that every successful

novel has five essential characters. These are:

     ○ *Love interest one*

    This is the main character. The one around

    which all the action takes place. It is usually

    the character who begins the story. In genres

    other than romance, they are the protagonist.

     ○ *Love interest two (and three, four ...)*

    This is (or are) the secondary main

    character/s. The one/s who will come in and

    disrupt the life of love interest one.

     ○ *Sidekick/best friend forever*

Every Wonder Woman needs her Etta Candy
(in the early comics, at least), every Batman
needs his Robin, and every love interest one
needs a BFF. So give them one.

o *Mentor*

This can be an older person, a wise person, a
silly person, or even a child. It is someone
who gives sage advice (intentionally or
otherwise) and directs the main love interest
in the right direction.

o *Antagonist*

This is the character/s, force/s, or event/s that
get in the way of the love interests being
together.

Jot down the five characters in your novel that apply
to this list and will fit your plot in the exercise below. You
don't have to have a clear idea of each of these characters at
this stage, but noting them down now will keep them in

your mind when it does come time to deepening your story later.

Exercise 9. What are the five characters your novel could have?

Love interest 1_____

Love interest 2 (and others)_____

_____

Sidekick/best friend forever_____

_____

Mentor_____

Antagonist_____

Further notes_____

_____

_____

That marks the end of your preliminary skills exercise questions. You can transfer your answers to the master worksheet in Appendix A and/or a notebook.

Before we move to the structural aspects of writing your breakout romance novel, there are two other important aspects to novel writing that need your attention: dialogue and writing mistakes.

Dialogue

Dialogue is more important to a story than many new writers realize. It can impart important information, advance a plot, heighten tension, set the tone, mood, and atmosphere of the story, and tell the reader a lot about each character. There are some basic techniques to follow when employing dialogue. Such as:

- *Listen to the way people speak, but don't write it verbatim*

  People use a lot of repetition, "um's," "ah's," and "er's" in their natural conversation. These can come across as irritating in books. A caveat: If this is a character trait, you can use it sparingly.

- *Avoid information dumping*

Information dumping is when you add too much information in one go, thus giving too much information to the reader in one lump. This can cause confusion. Don't add everything the reader needs to know in one piece of dialogue (or in the exposition/narrative sections, either). Keep dialogue snappy and short—unless a character is defined by their long-winded speeches!

o *Do not state the obvious*

I am sure you have all read books where a character says "as you know," or something similar. Readers will recognize this as an amateur attempt to get information across in a lazy way. Find other ways to get the information out (for example backstory, flashbacks, exposition, character actions, hints left around the house, overheard conversations, found items, anything random that feels wrong no matter how innocent it seems). If a character already knows something, it does not need to be pointed out that they know it.

- o *Watch your dialogue tags*

  Both using too many tags and adding a lot of adverbs should be avoided. It is another sign of amateur writing. "Said" or "asked" is fine. Only use other tag types if it gives extra meaning. The use of the occasional tag other than said or asked, judiciously used, makes a reader really pay attention.

- o *Punctuate correctly*

  Like everything with writing a novel, there is a way to set out your dialogue and this includes the way it is punctuated.

If you don't know how to do this, there are numerous resources online, such as *Grammar Girl*, that can help you. A professional editor is another option.

o *You don't need to add greetings and goodbyes to every conversation*
This gets annoying fast. In fact, you can leave them out as much as possible. Again, ignore this if it is your character's trait.

Furthermore, your dialogue must do *all* of the following:

o Move the story forward

o Reveal relevant information about the character (for example, insight into how the character feels or thinks, and what motivates him or her to act the way they do) o Help the reader understand the relationship between the characters.

Eleven of the most common writing mistakes

The following details the writing errors I regularly come across in my role as an editor. Avoid these and you will stand out from the slush pile in your submissions with stronger writing. Of course, rules are meant to be broken, but do so with caution, as well as the knowledge of *why* you are breaking them.

o *Show versus Tell*

This one is common. It is easy to write "Helen hated Clark." However, it is more interesting and enticing to the reader if you write "Helen drew on every ounce of willpower she had to stop herself from glaring in Clark's direction." Notice the difference? In the second version, we can *feel* the hatred along with Helen.

o *Active voice*

Passive writing is safe writing. This is why most beginning writers use it. To give your writing the oomph it deserves, switch to active voice as often as you can. As an example, passive voice: Nicole was running from the stranger. In the active voice, it would be: Nicole bolted from the stranger. Can you see the difference? Active voice makes it scarier and more immediate.

o *Lapses in point of view*

Go through your manuscript and look for a consistent point of view. Have you dropped into third person (he, she, and it) when you should be in first (I and me)? Or does your story head hop? Head hopping occurs when you start off a scene writing from one character's point of view then switch, without warning, to another character's thoughts or feelings. Don't do this. It confuses the reader and is a telltale amateur mistake.

o *Weak voice*

This most often happens when the writer is not confident in their writing or is trying too hard to copy another writer's style. Writing and reading a lot is the best and quickest way to strengthen your voice.

o *Clichés*

Delete all the clichés in your work as fast as a bat out of hell!

o *Similar sentence length throughout*

Varied sentence length makes your story more interesting, affect paces, and stops the reader from getting bored.

o *Lack of sense/s*

This is especially relevant to romance writers! You have five (or more, depending on who you ask) senses. Include them in your writing.

o *Adverbs*

Adverbs are those pesky words that end in "ly." They add nothing to your story (mostly). The general rule in writing is: Anything that doesn't add something needs to be cut. Get snipping.

o *Very and Just*

While you're cutting, make sure you delete "very" and "just." These are known as filler words. Filler words take up space and add nothing valuable to your writing. The same is true for filter words. Filter words describe the character seeing or thinking something, such as "see" and "think!" You also want to look out for words you overuse and rely on. These are known as "crutch words." There are plenty of other filler, filter, and crutch words you will need to look out for. However, very

and just are among the most common. A

more complete list is available at

www.fallinlovewithleigh.com/writingtips.

You can also carry out an internet search for

others.

- o *Thinking punctuation isn't important*

  You will be thanked if your editor can focus

  on your story rather than your punctuation.

  The more time an editor spends correcting

  your grammar and punctuation, the less they

  can spend on improving your story. Also,

  acquisitions editors will put your novel on

  the dreaded slush pile if they see hundreds of

  punctuation mistakes.

- o *Formatting*

  If you intend to send your manuscript to

  agents, editors, and publishers, you will need

  to have it formatted correctly. To find out

how to achieve this, check out my FREE

manuscript formatting checklist for authors

at my author services website

www.aklauthorsevices.com/checklists

Can you identify with any of these writing mistakes?
Are there any you would like to look out for in the future?
Note them in the space below.

Exercise 10. Writing mistakes I need to look out for:

Show versus Tell_____

_____

_____

Active voice_____

_____

_____

Lapses in point of view_____

_____

_____

Weak voice_____

_____

_____

Clichés_____

_____

_____

Similar sentence length throughout_____

_____

_____

Lack of sense/s_____

_____

_____

Adverbs_____

_____

_____

Very and Just (filler, filter, crutch words)_____

_____

_____

Thinking punctuation isn't important_____

_____

_____

Formatting_____

_____

_____

Further notes_____

_____

_____

We have now covered all the basics you need to become a successful romance author. You have also completed the first part of your novel outline— congratulations! With the preliminaries over, I want to reiterate that when it comes to writing romance, the most important part to focus on is *the journey to falling in love*, the lovers' journey. That is what draws the reader in—and keeps them reading.

You have taken the first steps by learning the preliminaries. We begin to follow the path in the next chapter as we delve into structure and the heart of *The Romance Novel Formula*.

Preliminaries checklist

o Have you completed the exercises in this chapter? Have you transferred your answers to the worksheet in Appendix A? If not, do that now.

o Have you made a note of any writing skill you want
to develop? Once you have, read, practice, and
attend workshops to aid you in that goal.

Chapter Two

Arcs

Every writer must understand structure. It is fantastic to have the preliminary skills needed to write a memorable novel, but if you have no structure to build it on, the story will fall apart.

What is structure?

The structure of any story includes the elements that keep it in a recognizable (and accepted) form to readers. Without structure, you have no story. There are three main parts to story structure. They are:

- Arcs
- Acts
- Beats

What is an arc?

An arc is the path of rising and falling action that occurs in a story. It can be visualized as a rainbow-shaped arc. There are a variety of arcs used in storytelling but the romance genre employs three: character arc, narrative arc, and relationship arc. The latter two will be discussed in chapter three. This chapter focuses on the character arc.

What is a character arc?

Character arc refers to the way the characters grow, change, and mature as the story unfolds. In the romance genre—I would argue more so than any other genre—the writer needs to be concerned with both the *internal* and *external* aspect of the character arc for ALL the main love interests … what was that about romance being an easy genre to write again?

The internal character arc is where you will see the most character growth and development. The external character arc is closely connected to the narrative arc, which will be expanded upon under the next heading. It is helpful to understand what your love interest's internal and external arcs are because they:

- o Create tension
- o Increase stakes
- o Are critical to character development
- o Are obstacles and challenges to your lovers' "happily-ever-after" or "happy-for-now"
- o Make your story stronger and more believable.

To get the most out of your internal and external character arcs, you will need to consider each character's G.M.C. (goal, motivation, conflict) as well as their F.N.F (fear, need, flaw).

The G.M.C. focuses mainly on external factors whereas the F.N.F brings the internal factors to light. G.M.C. was detailed in a fabulous book, *GMC: Goal, Motivation, and Conflict: The Building Blocks of Good*

Fiction, by Debra Dixon. F.N.F is something I developed to help me delve deeper into my character arcs.

For this chapter, you will once again complete individual exercises then utilize the G.M.C. worksheet included in Appendix B and the F.N.F. worksheet in Appendix C.

Let's look at each in more detail.

Goal, Motivation, Conflict

At this point, you want to think about the external plot points and the events that will happen in the story. These will help you define and refine your G.M.C. But first, what exactly are they?

Goal

The character's goal is precisely what it sounds like—the material, physical, or financial thing each main character wants to attain, obtain, or achieve. It is the *what* of your story. What does the character want? This has to be something external. The goal is an external object they think will fix their life or make them happy.

Of course, there are always internal factors going on, but our characters may or may not know that yet, so stay focused on the external goal for the moment.

Examples of goals in romance novels

From *Beautiful*

> For Bella: To earn a college degree which can help her get a job and gain financial independence.
>
> For Kit: To remain hidden in his cave from the outside world.

From *Pride and Prejudice*

> For Lizzie: It could be argued (and has been) that a "suitable" marriage is the main goal for all the unmarried characters. However, I feel Lizzie's is more specific to that goal: navigating her family's embarrassing behavior.

For Darcy: Never appearing inept, or less than what a gentleman should be.

From *Boyfriend Material*

For Lucien: To keep his job.

For Oliver: To have someone to take to his parents' wedding anniversary.

From the examples above, think about how your character goals might be similar or different. Then, write your notes below. You can transfer your answers to the G.M.C. worksheet in Appendix B once you are finished.

Exercise 11. What are your character goals?

Love interest 1 goals (what do they want?)_____

_____

_____

_____

_____

Love interest 2 goals (what do they want?)_____

_____

_____

_____

_____

Other love interests/further notes_____

_____

_____

_____

_____

Motivation

The motivation is the *why*. Why does the character want what they want? What is the driving force behind their goal, or the thing that keeps the character moving toward their goal? Again, it is usually an external motivation.

Examples of motivations in romance novels

From *Beautiful*

> For Bella: To get away from her controlling father and start a life that is her own.
>
> For Kit: Avoiding the glares and judgement of others and "keep the humans safe." There is also an element of penance to his self-confinement in the cave, in that he thinks he deserves to be punished for past mistakes.

From *Pride and Prejudice*

> For Lizzie: When Lizzie apologizes for her family's behaviors and exhorts her father to intervene on occasion, her motivation comes through. These actions are carried out so she can maintain her status and reputation, thereby allowing her to marry whomever she chooses and have a happy life.

> For Darcy: His family name, standing, and status are points of pride for him. He wants to maintain these by appearing a certain way to the general public.

From *Boyfriend Material*

> For Lucien: By having a "suitable" boyfriend, he can keep his job.

> For Oliver: To avoid questions about his relationship status and harassment over being single.

Look over these motivations and think about the *whys* of your own love interests. Why do they want what they want? Once you have your answers, write them in the space provided. You can note them in the appropriate place on your G.M.C. worksheet in Appendix B as well.

Exercise 12. What are your character motivations?
Love interest 1 motivations (Why does the character want it?)_____

_____

_____

_____

Love interest 2 motivations (Why does the character want it?)_____

_____

_____

_____

Other love interests/further notes_____

_____

_____

Conflict

The conflict is the main problem keeping the character from getting what they want. It encompasses the *why not* question. Think about what is stopping the character from their goal. Why can't they attain it? What is getting in the way? There are four main types of external conflict:

- *Character versus character*

  This is used to great effect in romance novels by having the love interests in direct competition with each other, or both having the same goal but for opposing reasons.

- *Character versus society*

  This can be seen via social and class differences as well as those of a more moral or ethical nature. An example of the latter could be a suffragette love interest.

- *Character versus nature*

  When elements, like animals, the weather, the environment, the land,

bushfires, and other natural phenomenon
are brought into the mix.

o *Character versus technology*
Killer cars and robots fall into this
category, but so does the technology,
innovations or developments that
threaten a person's job, home, and
livelihood.

A fifth conflict, character versus self, has not been
added because we are talking about external factors here,
and that one usually presents on an internal level.

Examples of conflict in romance novels

From *Beautiful*

Character versus society

Bella cannot enter society to complete her goal
while she is convalescing in the home of a beast. Kit
believes he will never be and doesn't deserve to be

accepted by human society, which becomes a

problem when he starts to have feelings for Bella.

From *Pride and Prejudice*

Character versus society

Lizzie and Darcy come from different social classes.

Hence, Lizzie cannot achieve her goal of a marriage

she chooses, and Darcy feels he will lose standing

by marrying her.

From *Boyfriend Material*

Character versus character

Lucien is in conflict with his boss who demands he

have an "appropriate boyfriend." Even though he

doesn't want a boyfriend, he is willing to have a

fake one to achieve his goal of keeping his job.

Oliver's parents are emotionally abusive and never

see him as "good enough". Having a partner is their

view of a successful life, so he agrees to a (fake-

real) boyfriend to appease them.

A note on relationship conflict

In the romance genre, you also need to think about the deeper *relationship conflict.* The conflict that keeps the love interests from getting what they want usually interferes with the relationship as well. Once you know the main conflict for your characters, you can expand this into how it prevents the love interests from getting into (and maintaining) a successful romantic relationship.

Examples of relationship conflict in romance novels

From *Beautiful*

> Character versus society
>
> A human dating a "beast" is scandalous even in this modern age. How Bella and Kit navigate this viewpoint is their deeper relationship conflict, especially for Kit.

From *Pride and Prejudice*

> Character versus society

There are others who have opinions on the potential marriage between Lizzie and Darcy—not all of them positive. These opinions affect Darcy more than Lizzie, to the point that he acknowledges it in his first, disastrous proposal to her.

From *Boyfriend Material*

Character versus character

Though they have agreed to the same pretense, they are doing so for different reasons. These come into conflict at different times, as does the "fakeness" of their relationship when real feelings develop.

Which conflict and relationship conflict represents your love interests? Read over the explanations and examples above then write your answers in the exercise below. Add them to your G.M.C. worksheet in Appendix B. This will complete the G.M.C. worksheet (yay! Another step you can tick off). You will then be ready to move onto your characters' F.N.F.

Exercise 13. What are your character and relationship conflicts?

Love interest 1 conflicts (Why can't the character get what they want?)_____

_____

_____

_____

Love interest 2 conflicts (Why can't the character get what they want?)_____

_____

_____

_____

Other love interests/further notes_____

_____

_____

What are the relationship conflicts keeping the love interests apart?_____

_____

_____

_____

_____

Fear, Need, Flaw.

This is where you start thinking about the internal aspects of your love interests' character arcs. The external parts of the arc are superficial whereas the internal parts add depth, relatability, and humanity. Fear, need, and flaw are the soul of your novel. But what exactly are they?

Fear

Even fictional characters have fears. By knowing the fears of each of your main characters, you have immediate insight into possible plot directions, conflicts, and growth points.

To pinpoint the character's fear, first think about their *whats*. What do they try to avoid? What can't they face? What do they put their head in the sand about? For instance, your love interest could fear being alone. They avoid it by engaging in a string of one-night stands.

Then, think about their *whys*. Why do they try to avoid it? Why can't they face it? Why do they put their head in the sand about it? The answer to this will show you what is referred to as the *character wound*. Something has happened to them that causes the fear. It could be something from their childhood. Using the previous instance, the character could fear being alone due to a number of instances in their childhood when their parent left them alone to fend for themselves for weeks on end. Or it could be a history of bad relationship choices, leading to mistrust. See how the wound drives the fear?

Keep in mind that the love interests may or may not be aware of their fear at the beginning of the novel, but they will need to acknowledge it by the end. To undergo a full transformation, the character must face their fear in some way.

Examples of fear in romance novels

From *Beautiful*

> For Bella: Uncertainty of her situation makes her afraid for her future. She is not sure what she will

face when she leaves Kit's home. Her wound (being

an abuse survivor) plays on this fear for her future.

For Kit: Rejection and being unlovable. He fears

that his "beast side" will be rejected by Bella just as

he is not accepted by the majority of the community

he hides from. His wound (being imprisoned and

treated like a subhuman) adds to the fear of his

unlovability.

From *Pride and Prejudice*

For Lizzie: She fears she will never find a suitable

partner due to her father's financial incompetence,

her mother's shrillness, and her sisters' multiple

social foibles. She would have seen "old maids"

throughout her life due to these reasons. A minor

wound that aggravates this fear is when she is

slighted by Mr. Darcy at the start of the novel.

For Darcy: He fears being seen as anything other

than a capable, upstanding citizen and ruining his

family's proud legacy. Which is why he butts heads

with Lizzie early on … she has no qualms about pointing out his defects! His wound stems from being played by his childhood companion, Mr. Wickham, on at least two occasions.

From *Boyfriend Material*

For Lucien: He fears having his private life blasted all over the news and social media. His wound is being seen as a drunken, idiotic fool who should not be taken seriously.

For Oliver: He fears being seen as weak in his parents' (and others') eyes. His wound comes from emotionally abusive parents who criticize his choices, behavior, and personality traits.

Additionally, both Lucien and Oliver fear they are too broken to be in a real relationship.

Ponder your character fears for a moment. What are they? Are the love interests aware of them or not? What is the wound that drives this fear? How can these fears be acknowledged and transformed by the end of your book?

Once you have the answers, note them in the space below

then transfer them to the F.N.F. worksheet in Appendix C.

Exercise 14. What are your character fears?

Love interest 1 fears (What does the character fear? What is
their wound?)_____

_____

_____

_____

_____

Love interest 2 fears (What does the character fear? What is
their wound?)_____

_____

_____

_____

_____

Other love interests/further notes_____

_____

_____

Need

The character's need is the lesson and behavioral change

they *need* to integrate into their lives for true growth and transformation. Knowing the character fear can give you a big clue to their need, which is why it is important to zero in on that first.

For instance, if your love interest fears rejection due to constant abandonment as a child (their wound), it can materialize in a flaw (more under the next subheading) of pushing people away before it can be done to them. This shows what they need is to heal their impulse to reject people, open themselves to others, and learn to trust. See how that comes together?

Like the fear, your characters may be unaware of their need. Alternatively, they may have had other characters point it out to them and have ignored or denied it, or they may be aware of it but are unsure how to resolve it (or don't want to because it would mean facing their fear).

If you're struggling to come up with a need, some of the most common ones include forgiveness, atonement, self-love, faith, trust, altruism, acceptance, prioritization, selflessness, responsibility, and redemption. Have a look at the examples below for more inspiration.

Examples of needs in romance novels

From *Beautiful*

> For Bella: She needs to learn to trust in herself as well as others. By doing this, she can overcome her fear regarding her future.
>
> For Kit: He needs two things: To love both sides of himself and give himself redemption for his past mistakes. That way, he will know he is worthy of Bella and the secret community he lives with.

From *Pride and Prejudice*

> For Lizzie: She needs to accept her tendency to act with prejudice so she can become more tolerant of other's flaws and make better judgments.
>
> For Darcy: He needs to take responsibility for the egotistical person he has been, which he does when he tells Lizzie he was "a selfish being all my life."

From *Boyfriend Material*

> For Lucien: He needs to have faith that others will
> not always expose his personal life to the press, and
> give his trust to people who prove themselves
> trustworthy.
>
> For Oliver: He needs to love himself enough to
> know that others will stand by him despite what he
> views as moments of weakness.
>
> It is time to list your love interests' needs. What

lesson and behavioral change will help them grow and

transform? Are your characters aware of their need or not?

Head to the exercise below to brainstorm then fill in your

F.N.F. worksheet in Appendix C.

Exercise 15. What are your character needs?

Love interest 1 needs (What does the character really

need?)_____

_____

_____

_____

_____

Love interest 2 needs (What does the character really
need?)_____

_____

_____

_____

_____

Other love interests/further notes_____

_____

_____

Flaw

Every character in your story must have at least one major

flaw (also known as the *character misbelief*). This flaw

keeps them stuck and unable to grow. It is most often a

misbelief they hold about themselves and/or life.

In romance, the character flaw includes the various

misconceptions about love that have occurred due to their

character wound. This can include past trauma, life

experience, failed relationships, bad parenting, physical or

psychological issues, and so forth.

These false beliefs drive your love interests' actions

and leave a lingering need, which is the true fix for the flaw.

This is why you must know what your characters need. The need fixes the flaw (and addresses the fear).

As a further guide, here are eleven of the most common character flaws:

- o Physical (such as a scar or physical condition that makes the character see themselves in a negative way)
- o Hypervigilance/overprotectiveness/having an unwavering opinion (usually from being a victim of crime, social injustice, or other bias)
- o Guilt and/or shame (over perceived failure/mistakes. To clarify: guilt is "I did something bad and feel terrible," while shame is "I am bad *because* I did something terrible")
- o Chronic mistrust
- o Not letting others get close/pushing them away

- Disillusionment/cynicism

- Arrogance/superiority complex (which is really an inferiority complex)

- Opinionated/judgmental

- Meddling in others' lives (often to avoid having to look at their own life)

- Too passive or aggressive

- Too controlling.

Examples of flaws in romance novels

From *Beautiful*

For Bella: She is too passive. By learning to trust herself and others, she becomes more assertive and makes positive decisions for her future.

For Kit: He is stuck in a cycle of guilt and shame and refuses to talk about difficult topics. When he loves both sides of himself and gives himself

redemption, he frees himself from this cycle.

From *Pride and Prejudice*

For Lizzie: Her prejudice leads her to make snap

judgments. When she acknowledges this about

herself, she is able to see the deeper sides to people

and open herself up to true love.

For Darcy: His pride means he has not always

considered the needs, values, and opinions of others.

Thus making him selfish. Having Lizzie call him out

for his behavior, he is challenged to think in a whole

new way—as does his lack of action toward Mr.

Wickham and its consequences.

From *Boyfriend Material*

For Lucien: His chronic mistrust means he takes his

true friends and the good aspects of his life for

granted. By paying attention to those who are there

for him and trusting that he is worthy of a real

relationship, he overcomes this flaw.

For Oliver: His controlling nature means he has little self-acceptance when he sees himself "fail". With some self-love and acceptance from those around him, this flaw recedes.

Now you can have a think about your love interests' flaws. Which of the examples given suit your characters the best? Once you have finished the exercise below, you can transfer your answer to the F.N.F. worksheet in Appendix C. You have now finished another step in your writing process!

Exercise 16. What are your character flaws?

Love interest 1 flaws (Why can't they resolve the fear and admit their true need?)_____

_____

_____

_____

_____

Love interest 2 flaws (Why can't they resolve the fear and admit their true need?)_____

_____

_____

_____

_____

Other love interests/further notes_____

_____

_____

Before moving on, make sure you can answer the questions in the checklist below for each of your main love interests.

Character arc checklist

Have you listed your characters'

1. Goals?

2. Motivations?

3. Conflicts?

4. Relationship conflicts?

5. Fears and wounds?

6. Needs?

7. Flaws?

Chapter Three

Acts and beats

In the previous chapter, you delved into your character arcs. This chapter provides a brief overview of the narrative arc and relationship arc, as well as the associated acts and beats that will help you with these.

What is a narrative arc?

The term *narrative arc* (also known as the *story arc*) refers to the sequence of events within which the overall story plays out. This is the place where you need to consider the main events of the story. In other words, it is the plot as a whole—this happens, then that happens, and it leads to this.

Acts come in handy with this part of your manuscript planning because they:

- o Keep your story on track

o   Ensure you are following the accepted
    structure of stories

o   Simplify the process so you don't get
    overwhelmed by the whole story in one go.

At this point, you might be thinking, "That's great … but what's an act and how can I use it?"

What is an act?

Many of you will be familiar with the concept of acts due to high school Shakespeare lessons, or whatever play your generation studied. In case you are not, here is my definition: acts are the way a narrative is cut up so that it flows in a logical and accepted format.

There are traditionally three acts (the beginning, middle, and end). However, some authors use four acts and others use five or more. *The Romance Novel Formula* employs five.

I chose this approach because many beginner writers get overwhelmed by a three-act structure. This is because the second/middle act makes up half of the manuscript. A large chunk. As such, it is where most new writers get stuck. I have found that breaking it down into smaller pieces makes it easier, minimizes pressure, and allows a much greater scope for originality, inventiveness, and creativity.

Furthermore, there are many proponents of the five-act structure: John Yorke (check out *Into the Woods*), Christopher Booker (detailed in *The Seven Basic Plots: Why We Tell Stories*), Gustav Freytag (seen in Freytag's Pyramid), and possibly even Shakespeare. According to Yorke, it also has ancient and classical origins, with Horace, Seneca the Younger, Terence, and Ben Johnson all using it.

Even so, you might find that using a traditional three-act structure works better for you. Or four. Or ten. That is fine. Ultimately, it doesn't matter how many acts you decide to work with, so long as you work with them!

Overview of the acts of *The Romance Novel Formula*

I refer to the five acts as:

- o Act 1. The Setup

- o Act 2. The Hookup

- o Act 3. The Ramp-up

- o Act 4. The Breakup

- o Act 5. The Makeup.

Each of these make up a rough percentage of the total book. I have provided a break down below to give you an idea of what this looks like:

- o Act 1. The Setup =

0-25% (the first 25% of the book)

- o Act 2. The Hookup =

25-50% (the next 25%)

*At this point, you will have half of your manuscript finished.

- o Act 3. The Ramp-up =

50-75% (the next 25%)

- o Act 4. The Breakup =

75-90% (the next 15%)

- o Act 5. The Makeup =

90-100% (the final 10% of the book)

The acts will be explained in more detail in the following chapters, so don't worry about having to memorize the above or understand everything right now. This is provided to prepare you for what is to come. Despite that, the names of the acts should give you an idea about the main purpose of each. Why don't you pause and take a moment to read over the titles of each act? How do you think they could correspond to an event in your book? In the space below, make a quick note about a possible event for each act based purely on the title of that act. A bonus of this exercise is that it will give you a rough outline to start writing your novel!

Exercise 17. Narrative arc (the acts).
Act 1 (The Setup)_____

_____

_____

_____

_____

_____

Act 2 (The Hookup)_____

_____

_____

_____

Act 3 (The Ramp-up)_____

_____

_____

_____

Act 4 (The Breakup)_____

_____

_____

_____

Act 5 (The Makeup)_____

_____

_____

_____

That takes care of the narrative arc. By completing this exercise, you have a rough outline with which to start writing your breakout romance novel. That's more than you had before you opened this book! The final arc to consider is the relationship arc. This is where the nitty-gritty of the lovers' journey, and *The Romance Novel Formula*, comes in. By digging deeper into this arc, you can expand upon the notes you've taken above.

What is a relationship arc?

The term *relationship arc* refers to the course of the relationship throughout the story. It is the essence of the lovers' journey.

Beats aid you at this stage of your story because they:

- o Give you an easy way to hit required plot points
- o Keep you on track (just like acts do for the narrative arc)
- o Can spark ideas
- o Can help you problem-solve and fill in plot holes

- Prevent the problems commonly associated with a second-act heavy structure

- Keep the romance at the fore.

Again, you might be wondering what a beat is and how it can achieve all of the above.

What is a beat?

Each act contains certain beats (also known as a *narrative beat*). These are specific events in the story that drive the plot, or subplots, forward. They help frame the typical structure of a story and can be thought of as the building blocks of acts. Every genre has them. In fact, the genre defines the type of beats needed.

There are many writing books out there, including those aimed at the romance genre. Some include a beat recipe, others have different ways of achieving the same thing, but none were suited to my needs. The beats I detail are those I've discovered by being a best-selling author and through the results of my research. This is why *The Romance Novel Formula* is especially pertinent for those who want to be romance authors.

To break this down further, there can be one beat per scene or chapter, but there can also be multiple beats per scene or chapter … and there can be none. It all depends on the type of story you want to tell and the word length.

Moreover, some beats don't need to be hit in order. Of course, you can't have the final beat in the first chapter, or the story would be over, but there is some room for movement. Yes, it gets confusing, but the more you write, the more you will get a feel for when the beats need to be hit. For now, if you are a newbie, stick to the beats in order as much as possible.

Either way, the beats are the same regardless of the romance subgenre you are writing in. They also do not change whether your lovers are gay, straight, alien, ménage, polyamorous, and anything else your imagination can bring into being.

The Romance Novel Formula contains eleven main beats, all of which will be explained and expanded upon in the subsequent chapters. In Appendix D, there is a beat sheet template for you to use. The template can be adapted depending on whether you are a plotter, pantser, or plantser.

For instance, you can:

- o Make an outline of your entire story before you begin (best for plotters)
- o Refer to it during the writing process to make sure you are hitting the required markers (best for pantsers)
- o Write a rough outline then refer to it during the writing process (best for plantsers)
- o Use it at the final draft stage to ensure you have included all the beats (excellent for all writers).

Overview of the beats of *The Romance Novel Formula*

ACT 1: The Setup

1. Introduction of the first love interest

2. First interaction

3. Something forces them together.

ACT 2: The Hookup

4. Misguided or denial of feelings

5. Feelings get harder to deny.

ACT 3: The Ramp-up

6. Confession of feelings

7. Reaction to confession.

ACT 4: The Breakup

8. Rejection of relationship

9. Misery.

ACT 5: The Makeup

10. Come together

11. H.E.A. or H.F.N.

Much like we did for the acts, you are going to pause now and brainstorm some ideas for your novel based on the titles of the beats. They don't have to be ideas you end up using in your final draft. This is simply an exercise to get your brain thinking about your story and showing you that you CAN write a romance. Each exercise I'm taking you through is designed to build your story so you have something solid to work with, as opposed to a wishy-washy idea that is stuck in your head. What you write down here will be expanded upon in upcoming chapters.

Exercise 18. Relationship arc (the beats).
Beat 1 (Introduction of the first love interest)_____

_____

_____

_____

Beat 2 (First interaction)_____

_____

_____

_____

Beat 3 (Something forces them together)_____

_____

_____

_____

Beat 4 (Misguided or denial of feelings)_____

_____

_____

_____

Beat 5 (Feelings get harder to deny)_____

_____

_____

_____

Beat 6 (Confession of feelings)_____

_____

_____

_____

Beat 7 (Reaction to confession)_____

_____

_____

Beat 8 (Rejection of relationship)_____

_____

_____

_____

Beat 9 (Misery)_____

_____

_____

_____

Beat 10 (Come together)_____

_____

_____

_____

Beat 11 (H.E.A. or H.F.N.)_____

_____

_____

_____

A note on scenes and sequels

Just as beats are the building blocks of acts, scenes and sequels help you to hit your beats.

You know you have written a scene when your character attempts to achieve their goal, or something important happens. As such, the purpose of a scene is to drive the conflict or plot forward and ramp up the tension. Sequels are reactions and/or decisions related to the scene. A simple way to remember the difference is: Scenes are the action and sequels are the reaction, or effect of the action.

In romance, you could have a scene where the first love interest is applying for a promotion but is rejected (their attempt to achieve their goal). In the scene's sequel, you can show them feeling depressed (the reaction) until they decide to snap out of it and try again (a decision).

You will also have passages of writing in your story that are neither scenes nor sequels. For instance, you could have description (of a person, place, or thing), exposition (background details or information), and backstory (parts of the characters' pasts that are relevant to their present). These are necessary elements that move the story forward and give your reader a break from constant action-reaction.

To summarize, your scenes and sequels help you hit your beats, which fill your acts, to create the perfect structure for your breakout romance novel.

This completes the overview of the beats that make up the relationship arc/lovers' journey and the acts of the narrative arc. The acts and beats will now be expanded upon in the following chapters.

Chapter Four

Act 1

How long should Act 1 be?

Act 1 should make up the first twenty-five percent of the book.

The purpose of Act 1

I refer to Act 1 as the *setup* because the writer's job is to set up the ensuing story for the reader. It sounds easy, but there are many purposes to Act 1 that need to be considered. Some of these include:

- o Showing the ordinary life of the love interests
- o Hinting at the theme/s and dramatic question (more on this soon)
- o Showing the G.M.C. and F.N.F of the love interests
- o Introducing all main characters

o   Showing the trope/master plot/archetypes

o   Hinting at the character, narrative, and

    relationship arcs

o   Increasing reader empathy for the love

    interests

o   Increasing reader desire for the love interests

    to unite

o   Preparing the transition into the second act,

    which is when the romance will ramp up.

As you can see from the above list, the first act holds a lot of the story on its shoulders. It can seem overwhelming when you are first starting out, but as I've said before, it gets easier the more you write. You can also work on one aspect with each draft you write instead of trying to cram everything in at one time.

But before any of that, you need a beginning.

How do I start the first act?

As a general rule, start your story with the person you want the reader to identify with the most. Readers tend to sympathize with the first character they are introduced to, so make sure you choose wisely. In the romance genre, it should be one of your love interests.

Once you've decided on this character, you can write your first sentence. Use your first sentence to hook the reader into your story—this is called the *opening hook*. There are several ways to write a successful opening hook. The most common are:

- o *Leave an unanswered question*

  An example from William Goldman's fairytale romance, *The Princess Bride*: "This is my favorite book in all the world, though I have never read it." Tell me that opening doesn't have you asking questions and wanting to read more! Why is it his favorite book … and how does he know if he has never read it? Questions, questions, and more questions.

- *Hint at the theme*

  You can do this in a playful, serious, or even an ironic manner, such as the famous opener from the classic romance novel, *Pride and Prejudice*: "It is a truth universally acknowledged, that a single man in possession of a good fortune, must be in want of a wife." This hints at the theme of marriage that will permeate the novel.

- *State an interesting character opinion*

  This differs from a hint at the theme because it gives us a glimpse into the character's personality rather than the theme. In *Boyfriend Material*, Alexis Hall opens with Luc's opinion: "I've never seen the point of fancy-dress parties." This works because those who agree with this viewpoint will

want to know if his reasons for hating them
align with their own and those who love
fancy dress will want to read on to find out
how someone can't see the point of them.

o   *Dive straight into the action*

Again, this can be something explosive
(literally) or it can be more subtle.
Whichever you use, it needs to be
interesting. Take this opening line from Irene
Hannon's romantic suspense novel, *Against
All Odds*: "Sir? I think you need to hear
this." This simple statement tells us that
something has happened (action) and gets us
wondering what based on the tone and
atmosphere created. See how even subtle
action can draw you in?

o   *Use dialogue*

This is used less commonly in other genres,
but often in romance. Again, the

conversation must be interesting and believable. One of my favorite dialogue openers comes from the contemporary romance novel, *The Notebook,* by Nicholas Sparks: "Who am I?" Yes, self-dialogue counts! This opening is brilliant because it also hints at one of the themes (unconditional love even through memory loss).

o *Use non-linear time*

Stephenie Meyer used this technique well in her paranormal romance, *Twilight,* when she started it with, "I'd never given much thought to how I would die—though I'd had reason enough in the last few months." Wow! This makes you curious about what has happened to this girl in the past months to have her thinking about her death.

o *Something shocking or unexpected*

Think of this one from Diana Gabaldon's historical romance, *Outlander*: "It wasn't a very likely place for disappearances, at least at first glance." Whoa! The reader realizes there is something weird going on in Inverness and wants to know why people are disappearing.

- *Parallels to the love interest's life*

  For instance, in *Beautiful*, this is my opening line: "The fox squirrel skittered back as I approached the wire cage. *He's still suspicious of humans.*" As you read on, you discover that Bella is in her own metaphorical cage and is also suspicious of humans. There are also parallels to Kit's life, so this opening works on a couple of levels.

Have a look at your opening sentence. Does it fit into any of these categories? If not, how can you rework it so it does? Have you chosen the right love interest to start this story? Experiment with love interests and hook options to see which one stands out.

A cautionary note here. The first line can trip a lot of writers up. They spend so much time crafting the perfect beginning … then nothing. Don't get so stuck on your opening that your forget about the rest of the story. Play around and experiment, then move on. You can always come back to it. The point is to get a complete draft finished before you worry about tidying it up in subsequent drafts. Jot down some possible opening sentences in the following exercise then you can work on your first act and its beats.

Exercise 19. Opening sentence.

Leave an unanswered question_____

_____

_____

_____

_____

Hint at the theme_____

_____

_____

_____

_____

State an interesting character opinion_____

_____

_____

_____

Dive straight into the action_____

_____

_____

_____

Use dialogue_____

_____

_____

_____

Use non-linear time_____

_____

_____

_____

Something shocking or unexpected_____

_____

_____

_____

_____

Parallels to the love interest's life_____

_____

_____

_____

_____

How many beats make up the first act?

According to *The Romance Novel Formula,* there are three beats in the first act. They are the *introduction of the first love interest, the first interaction,* and *something forces them together.*

Beat 1—Introduction of the first love interest

Give the reader a *glimpse* into the ordinary life of this character. Where do they live or work? What is their usual routine? What is their personality? A warning here: you don't want to draw out the beginning with too many mundane details or exposition because readers will get bored. Hence the inclusion of the word glimpse. Make it interesting for the reader.

For this beat, you will need to:

o *Begin building his/her/their everyday world*

Show them at home, work, and/or play (á la Jessica Brody's suggestion) to get the reader invested and interested. As home, work and play are the three areas of life most of us can relate to, letting the reader see your characters in these settings can cement them into their minds. It can also make the characters more relatable, real, and three-dimensional.

o *Make sure you introduce the main character as soon as possible*

You want the reader to connect with them immediately. Also keep in mind that the first character you introduce is usually the one the reader will root for, so be careful if you introduce an antagonist first!

o *Ensure you hook the reader*

The hook can be an interesting word, phrase, or sentence that draws the reader into your story straight away. See above for the list of most common hooks.

o *Character, action, setting, theme, question*

On the above point, to further grab your reader, make sure you include at least two of the following in the first paragraph: Character, action, setting, theme, dramatic question.

o *Speaking of the dramatic question*

While it *can* be a good idea to pose the dramatic question (more on this soon) in the first paragraph, it is not necessary and can wait until later on in act one … just make sure you have it appear somewhere in act one.

Examples of the first beat in romance novels

From *Beautiful*

> Bella-Rosa Amato lives in a mansion and has an outwardly glamourous life. However, she is unhappy in her home life due to her father's controlling and abusive behavior towards her.

From Pride and Prejudice

> Witty and opinionated Elizabeth "Lizzie" Bennet is introduced in her interactions with her family.

From Boyfriend Material

> Lucien is at a fancy-dress party he doesn't want to be at. He is the son of a famous, aging rocker who has had nothing to do with him. He is socially awkward.

In the space below, make some notes for your first beat. Once you have the ideas down, you can start writing them into your first draft.

Exercise 20. Beat 1—Introduction of the first love interest

*You can refer to the notes you made for this beat during exercise 18 (Relationship arc).

How can you show your first love interest at home, work, and play?_____

_____

_____

_____

_____

How can you introduce the main character as soon as possible?_____

_____

_____

_____

_____

How can you include character, action, setting, and theme in your first paragraph?_____

_____

_____

_____

_____

You now (hopefully) have a rough first beat so it is time to work on your story's second beat. When you have all of your beats, you will need to develop your story so that one beat leads naturally to the next. For now, work on each individual beat.

Beat 2—First interaction

This is known in non-romance circles as the *inciting incident*. In romance, this is commonly known as the *meet cute* and refers to the event that sets the romance up. This usually occurs within the first fifteen percent of the book; however, as already stated, there is always room to wiggle. Having said that, readers will get impatient the longer you draw it out.

I have renamed this beat because, in my research for this book, I found that there was often no meet cute. At least not according to the meaning typically given for that term: a cute way the love interests meet. In fact, often the couples had a disastrous first meeting, or they already knew each other (hence the "meet" was invalid). Despite that, there is always something that sparks an interest, even if that interest is contempt.

Therefore, I call this beat the *first interaction* to cover the love interests who do know each other, as well as those who don't. As mentioned above, the first interaction can be a positive one (a traditional meet cute) or a negative one (a meet ugly). This applies whether the love interests know each other already or not.

For this beat, you will need to:

o *Introduce the second (and subsequent) love interest/s*

If the second love interest has not already been brought into the story, they need to be at this point (otherwise, there can be no first interaction!).

It does not need to be as drawn out as our introduction to the main love interest. The details of their life can be revealed as we, and the characters, get to know them.

However, you can give the reader a more detailed look at their life if you choose. The latter is the path I tend to take in my novels, as I like my readers to have a good sense of both of my characters before I get them to meet. If you do go with this option, you must flesh out their lives as much as you did for love interest one. And remember not to drone on too long.

You can do the same for each subsequent love interest, but be careful once you reach a third person/alien/etc. because this can start getting confusing and repetitive for the reader.

o *The interaction*

Choose whether you are going to have your love interests meet in a cute or ugly way, then make it happen.

Examples of the second beat in romance novels

From *Beautiful*

Kit rescues Bella from being attacked. Although this meeting happens under tragic circumstances, it is still considered a meet cute meet because they are happy about the meeting.

From Pride and Prejudice

The "proud and arrogant" Mr. Fitzwilliam Darcy unwittingly insults Lizzie when she overhears him refusing to dance with her because she is "tolerable, but not handsome enough to tempt me" at the Meryton ball. This is a famous meet ugly scene.

From Boyfriend Material

After being asked by their mutual friend, Oliver Blackwood agrees to meet up with Lucien. They have met before, each time disastrous. This starts out as a meet ugly due to their previous interactions with each other, but becomes a meet cute due to their mutual awkwardness.

You can move onto the accompanying exercise to jot down your ideas for this beat. Like the previous exercise, the one given below will help you write the

second beat for your rough draft.

Exercise 21. Beat 2—First interaction.

*You can refer to the notes you made for this beat during exercise 18 (Relationship arc).

How can you introduce the other love interest/s?_____

_____

_____

_____

_____

_____

_____

What are some ideas for a meet cute?_____

_____

_____

_____

_____

_____

What are some ideas for a meet ugly?_____

_____

_____

_____

_____

You are almost finished the rough draft of your first act. I hope you are getting as excited as I am for you! Let's move onto the third beat.

Beat 3—Something forces them together

This is an external situation that will force the love interests to spend time together. It could be a work situation, mutual friends needing them for a project/wedding, literally being stuck somewhere together, or a natural disaster that has them in lockdown. As long as it is something *external*, you can let your imagination run wild.

For this beat, you will need to:

    ○ *Bait the hook!*

You will need to include at least once scene (and possibly a sequel) that forces the love interests together in some way. This will prepare the love interests for the events of the second act, which will hook them up.

The first three beats are focused mostly on the individual journeys of the love interests, and setting them up for their life-changing walk on the lovers' journey. The rest of the acts and beats will take into consideration the growth and connection of all parties because that is what the lovers' journey is about. As the love interests leave the first act, they will start a new adventure on the path to love in Act 2.

Some other writing craft guides refer to this as "entering their new world" or "stepping over the threshold."

Examples of the third beat in romance novels

From *Beautiful*

Bella has been injured during the attack, so she must stay with Kit in his home while she recovers.

From Pride and Prejudice

Lizzie's beloved sister, Jane, falls ill on her journey to visit Caroline Bingley, her love interest's sister, at nearby Netherfield hall. Out of concern for her sister, Lizzie walks to the house and remains to care for Jane. As Darcy is also at the house, they are forced to spend time together and interact.

From Boyfriend Material

Lucien needs an "acceptable" boyfriend to keep his job and clean up his public appearance.

Oliver needs a boyfriend to placate his critical parents.

Time to make some notes for your third beat. Then, write your third beat in your first draft.

Exercise 22. Beat 3—Something forces them together.
*You can refer to the notes you made for this beat during exercise 18 (Relationship arc).

How will you force your love interests together?_____

_____

_____

_____

_____

Now that you've finished the third beat, look over what you've written. Can you detect the common setup elements in the examples given? Does your first act deliver something similar? Are your setup beats as obvious, original or notable as the examples? Go back and make any changes now.

You're almost done, I promise. But before you move to the second act and its beats, there are a couple of other important points to note.

The importance of the first chapter

Many creative writing coaches, myself included, laud the importance of the first chapter. Readers need to be engaged with what they are reading from the first word, but overall, it is the first chapter that will decide whether they keep reading or not. In the first chapter, make sure you:

- o Introduce the protagonist (love interest one) and as many main characters as you can

- o Set up the basics of the story

- Hint at/show the G.M.C. of the first love interest

- Hint at/show the F.N.F of the first love interest

- Show the reader *why* they should care about the love interest and story you are about to tell.

How do I end the first act?

The first act is all about setting up the ordinary world of the love interests and the possibility of them entering a romance. End the first act when the love interests are about to embark on a new world together.

Also ensure you end with a closing teaser, hook, or mini-cliff hanger, which leads into the second act and encourages the reader to continue. It can be a question, thought, or action that makes the reader want to keep turning the pages and can relate to the romance, main plot, or subplot. It is good practice to end all your chapters and acts this way, but is not always necessary if the story and writing are solid.

Use the following exercise as a way to plan your first act ending. Then, write it in your first draft.

Exercise 23. Ending the first act.
What new world are the love interests about to enter?_____

_____

_____

_____

_____

What closing teaser, hook, or mini-cliff hanger would work well?_____

_____

_____

_____

_____

As mentioned earlier, you need to ensure that the beats all lead onto each other in a sensible way. Take some time now to rework your first act. **That's it. You've completed the first act of your first draft.**

Congratulations!

Act 1 checklist

1. Have a look at your manuscript. Have you got a clearly definable beat 1? Do we know something about the everyday world of your main character? What is their job or home life like?

2. Have you got an intriguing opening hook?

3. Turn to beat 2. Is your second beat a "meet cute," "meet ugly," or something in between? Is it obvious? Does it occur within the first fifteen percent of the book?

4. Does your third beat give your love interests a strong reason to be forced into proximity?

5. Have you ensured there is equal representation in your novel between the love interests (do they have roughly equal pages devoted to them)?

6. Is it as close to twenty-five percent of your book's total page count as possible?

7. Have you made a relationship between the love interests seem likely?

8. Has a transition into a possible romance been set up well enough?

9. Do you have an intriguing closing hook?

10. Does your first chapter and first act encourage the reader to keep going?

Chapter Five

Act 2

How long should Act 2 be?

Act 2 should make up the next twenty-five percent of the book. By the end of this act, you should have half of your novel's first draft finished. How exciting is that!

The purpose of Act 2

I refer to Act 2 as the hookup because the focus in this section is to get the main love interests together—to hook them up. If you have completed the setup part of Act 1 correctly, your Act 2 should flow, and the reader should believe that a connection between the lovers is authentic and in line with the situation.

In this act, you want your love interests to go on dates, spend time together, and get to know each other better. To delve deeper, you need to:

- Progress the romance between the love interests. They need to take at least one step toward being together—first official date, holding hands, that sort of thing—by the end of Act 2

- Foreshadow the black moment (more on this later)

- Show the love interests trying to overcome their internal and external conflicts

- Advance both subplots and the main plot

- Respond to the closing hook of Act 1.

How do I start the second act?

The first thing to do is to have the characters react to the closing hook of the first act. They are moving from their old lives into the possibility of a new life with each other.

The next exercise can help you with starting your second act. You know the deal by now. Once you've finished your notes, use them to write the second act

opening in your first draft.

Exercise 24. Starting the second act.

How can your love interests react to the closing teaser,

hook, or mini-cliff hanger from the first act?_____

_____

_____

_____

_____

We can now move onto the beats. The process is the

same as the one you followed for the first act. Complete the

exercises, write your individual beats, then rework what

you've written into a cohesive, sensible piece of writing.

How many beats make up the second act?

According to *The Romance Novel Formula,* there are two

beats in the second act: *denial of feelings* and *feelings get*

harder to deny.

In this act, you will set up subplots and have the

love interests go on dates and spend time together. Even

though it might seem like there is little going on for such a large chunk of the manuscript, you will soon find there is a lot to cover.

Beat 4—Denial of/misguided feelings

To hit this beat, you will show one or more of the lovers denying their attraction and/or growing feelings for the other love interest/s. This can include believing the other love interest/s has no feelings for them. That would be classed as "misguided feelings."

For this beat, you will need to:

- o *Show that denial is not just a river in Egypt!*

  Bad pun aside, you have to show the love interests struggling with feelings or positive opinions about the other person. They might acknowledge the feelings or thoughts, but quickly dismiss them. They will list all the reasons why "hooking up" would not be a good idea. Some of these reasons might have nothing to do with the love interest (i.e. it could stem from the flaw or conflict). Also, the denial can be on one person's side, or all of the involved love interests.

When the denial has been convincingly established, events will need to happen that make the next beat (feelings get harder to deny) believable. But first, here are some examples of the fourth beat to get your brain working, then you can complete the following exercise for your own ideas.

Examples of the fourth beat in romance novels

From Beautiful

Bella tells herself that her growing feelings for Kit are based on gratitude and the fact he saved her life. Kit tells himself that he cannot allow himself to feel anything for Bella because she will reject him based on his looks and his past. They spend every day together because she is injured and cannot go anywhere (*forced to spend time together* setup in the previous act).

From Pride and Prejudice

Lizzie continues her prejudice against Darcy by easily believing lies his foe, Mr. Wickham, spreads about him. Darcy, on the other hand, finds it increasingly difficult to forget Lizzie's "fine eyes" no matter how hard he tries. As Darcy's best friend, Bingley, has an undeniable interest in Lizzie's sister, Jane, they are all forced to cross paths and spend time together, thereby learning more about each other.

From Boyfriend Material

Lucien believes Oliver is too good for him. Oliver confirms this thought when Lucien tries to kiss him, and Oliver says he "reserves that for people he likes." They go on pretend dates due to the fake relationship agreement; *forced to spend time together* setup in the previous act.

Exercise 25. Beat 4—Denial of/misguided feelings
*You can refer to the notes you made for this beat during exercise 18 (Relationship arc).
How will your love interests deny their feelings or believe that the other person has no interest in them?_____

_____

_____

_____

_____

_____

_____

It's the time to transfer your notes from here and write them as a section in your first draft. Then, move to beat 5. Keep going, you are almost finished the second act.

Beat 5—Feelings get harder to deny

The more time the love interests spend together, the harder their attraction and/or growing connection is to deny. All the reasons the love interests believe a romance could not work with the other person are still there, but the emotions and feelings are getting in the way (or, rather, clearing the path to true love, personal fulfillment, and character growth. But your characters don't know that yet!).

For this beat, you will need to:

- o *Show the love interests struggling with their feelings*

  It is fine if you focus on one character's struggle; however, because this is a romance novel and you are taking your characters on the lovers' journey, it is stronger if you include all love interests in this beat. Of course, you can show it in different scenes—and chapters—so long as it is there. You can also have one love interest being in absolute denial while another knows they have feelings, but still cannot accept any sort of romantic relationship can develop.

Further, this struggle can be shown as an internal or physical struggle, or both. Some examples of the former include thinking about all the reasons it can't work, refusing to linger on the attraction when it arises, or trying to reason away feelings. Physical examples can include berating themselves out loud, pacing, maintaining a physical distance from the love interest/s, and avoiding eye contact.

o *Show the love interests accepting their feelings*

Regardless of the effort the love interests put in to continue to deny their feelings, the feelings will continue to grow. Ultimately, at least one of the love interests will not be able to deny it anymore and come to accept the place the other person (or people) has in their lives and heart. This can be classed as the *mirror moment* in romance; when the possibility of a romance with the love interest/s seems possible.

Need some examples? I'm so glad you asked.

Examples of the fifth beat in romance novels

From Beautiful

The more time they spend together, the more Kit and Bella realize their feelings are based on something real. Kit tries to get over them because he still does not believe Bella could love him as he really is, whereas Bella is starting to accept them as real.

From Pride and Prejudice

> While visiting her good friend, Charlotte, at
> Rosing's Park (the grand home of Darcy's aunt),
> Lizzie runs into Darcy and they spend more time
> together. Darcy finds it even harder to deny how
> he feels about Lizzie.

From Boyfriend Material

> Lucien thinks about how "nice, safe, and right"
> it feels with Oliver.

See how in these examples the love interests have moved from their old lives and embarked on a new one that involves each other, even though one or all aren't ready to accept that yet? This is what your second act and its associated beats should achieve. It is time to get your writing hands warmed up with notes for your fifth beat.

Exercise 26. Beat 5—Feelings get harder to deny

*You can refer to the notes you made for this beat during exercise 18 (Relationship arc).

How will you show your love interests struggling with their feelings? Love interest 1_____

_____

_____

_____

_____

Love interest 2_____

_____

_____

_____

_____

Other love interests/further notes_____

_____

_____

_____

_____

In what ways can you show your love interests accepting their feelings? Love interest 1_____

_____

_____

_____

_____

Love interest 2_____

_____

_____

_____

_____

Other love interests/further notes_____

_____

_____

Are you happy with your notes? Great. Write up this beat in your first draft.

Once again, before you can jump to the third act and its beats, there are some other pertinent markers for the second act. The first of these is the G.T.K.Y. stage.

What is the G.T.K.Y. stage?

These two beats will also need to encompass what I call the _G.T.K.Y._ (getting to know you) stage. Some of the other romance beat sheets say three dates (this is anything that denotes spending time together, whether the love interests consider them a date or not) need to happen at this point of the story.

However, my research showed often there were only one or two moments the couple spent together, and sometimes there were a lot more. Hence, use the three dates as a guideline only. Don't force an extra two dates into the story if one would make it stronger. Likewise, don't cut down on the time they spend together if it moves the story along.

Instead, focus on the love interests learning the basics about each other—what their external goals, wishes, and dreams are (and if that is in conflict with their own). Add in some personal history (do they have an ex who cheated on them? A parent that has died?).

This is also where you want to ensure you are showing the *five bonds* (physical, emotional, mental, sexual, and spiritual) discussed in chapter one, if you haven't already. You will need to put your characters in situations that show these bonds growing (more on this in the exercise below so don't worry about it yet).

The G.T.K.Y. process can, and should, enlighten the love interests as to why they behave the way they do and give them a clearer understanding of personalities and traits. They will start seeing qualities in the other that make them change their initial impression of them (if it was a meet ugly) or reinforce it (in the case of a meet cute). The doubts or views they had about the love interest and/or relationships in general will shift, even as they continue to deny this.

Exercise 27. The G.T.K.Y. stage.
How can your love interests spend time together and get to know each other? It's always great to think outside the box here_____

_____

_____

_____

_____

_____

Go back to your preliminaries worksheet and peruse the notes you made under exercise 8 (where's the bond?). How can you use what you wrote down to create bonds between your love interests? Come up with at least one idea for physical, emotional, mental, sexual, and spiritual_____

_____

_____

_____

_____

_____

_____

Open up your first draft and add the above elements into your second act.

Avoiding the dreaded *saggy middle*

The saggy middle is a term given to books lacking interesting developments in the second act (of a third-act structure). Now, as you are using a five-act structure instead of a third-act structure, you can avoid that dilemma by making sure you hit the beats. This is one of the other benefits using a five-act structure has over a third-act structure.

How do I end the second act?

As the main purpose of the second act is to hook up your characters, it ends when the feelings of at least one of the love interests can no longer be denied and they are ready to accept the way they feel. Have a think about your love interests. Do you know who will accept their feelings?

Keep in mind that the third act is all about ramping everything up—feelings, events, conflicts, subplots—so end the second act on the cusp of all of these. Again, finishing with a hook at this point will encourage readers to continue.

Complete the following exercise then use what you've written to end the second act in your first draft.

Exercise 28. Ending the second act.
Which love interest will accept their feelings? Why? Is this a natural outcome from the story so far?_____

_____

_____

_____

_____

_____

_____

What interesting hook could you use to encourage readers
to continue?_____

_____

_____

_____

_____

_____

You are now at the point you reached in the first act
where you must tidy up your beats to ensure they lead onto
each other in a sensible way. Take some time to rewrite
before moving on. **Can you believe you are officially
halfway through your first draft? Well done.**

Act 2 checklist

- o   How does the fourth beat show up in your
     manuscript? Are the love interests denying their
     connection? Is it a traditional "denial of feelings" or
     a "misguided feelings" situation?

- o   How do you show the beat 5 feelings getting harder
     to deny?

o Do your love interests spend time together? What are their G.T.K.Y. scenes? Do you use these scenes to show their five bonds?

o Have you ensured there is equal representation between the love interests (do they have roughly equal pages devoted to them)?

o Is your second act as close to twenty-five percent of your book's total page count (not word count) as possible? This should be roughly fifty percent of your complete manuscript.

o Have you made a romantic relationship between the love interests seem believable as well as likely?

o Do you have an opening hook as well as a closing hook?

o Does your closing hook encourage the reader to keep going?

Chapter Six

Act 3

How long should Act 3 be?

Act 3 makes up the next twenty-five percent of the book.

The purpose of Act 3

I call the third act the ramp-up because this is the section of your manuscript where you need everything—the main plot, character G.M.C., character F.N.F, subplots, and the romance—to ramp up. To achieve this, make sure you:

- Deepen the relationship between the love interests. They should be showing signs of moving toward a commitment of some kind during this act
- Heighten the G.M.C.
- Heighten the F.N.F.
- Progress all plots

- Foreshadow the inevitable breakup that will happen in act four.

How do I start the third act?

The second act ended with at least one love interest accepting they had feelings for the other love interest/s. Now, they need to decide what to do about it.

Just because they have admitted to themselves that there is more going on for them, it does not necessarily mean they want to jump into a romantic relationship. They might decide it would be best to get rid of their feelings through asking the love interest/s for a one-night stand, or by diving into work, or by assuming the feelings will fade over time.

They might also believe the other love interest/s does not feel the same (misguided feelings) or could be spooked if they admit how they feel. Hence, they think it would be better to keep the knowledge to themselves until they are certain of where they stand.

The other option is that they *do* want a romantic relationship with the love interest/s and decide to admit it.

Which will they choose? That is up to you, and is part of the fun that comes with writing romance that other genres miss out on. Any of these possibilities makes for an interesting (hopefully) third act. The individual reactions and decisions of all love interests surrounding this knowledge will form the basis of most of this act. Once again, you will achieve this through the beats for this act. Before you can dive into the beats, you need to work on your third act beginning.

Exercise 29. Starting the third act.
How can your love interests react to the knowledge of their feelings from the second act? Will they tell the other love interest/s? Will they plunge into work to forget? What else could they do?_____

_____

_____

_____

_____

Use these notes to write the opening of your third act in your first draft. Then, you can learn more about the beats.

How many beats make up the third act?

According to *The Romance Novel Formula,* there are two beats in the third act. They are the *confession of feelings* and *reaction to confession.*

Beat 6—Confession of feelings

One or all love interests admit to feelings and/or the desire to enter some form of relationship or commitment. At a minimum, they must have admitted how they feel and what they want to themselves.

For this beat, you will need to:

- *Confess!*

  As the name of this beat states, you will need to add a scene where you have the character/s admitting their growing feelings.

This confession can be to themselves, a trusted friend whom they ask for advice, or to the love interest/s. Which of these options best suits your characters and the story you are telling?

Examples of the sixth beat in romance novels

From Beautiful

Bella hints at her feelings for Kit, so Kit feels confident enough to admit his feelings to her.

From Pride and Prejudice

While Lizzie is visiting her newly married best friend, Charlotte, Darcy barges in uninvited and proposes. He admits how much he "ardently admires and loves" her while also lamenting the "inferiority of her connections."

From Boyfriend Material

After Lucien freaks out and breaks up with Oliver over a news headline that brought back traumatic memories, he shows up at Oliver's home and explains why he freaked out. Oliver takes Lucien back while admitting he "has something he cares about more than his job." Lucien admits he has feelings for Oliver and vice versa.

These examples share the common trait of this beat—confession—but they play out in unique, story-specific ways. Think about your own story then make some notes below.

Exercise 30. Beat 6—Confession of feelings
*You can refer to the notes you made for this beat during exercise 18 (Relationship arc).
How can you make your confession unique and interesting as well as story-specific?_____

_____

_____

Take your ideas and work them into your first draft.

Okay, one or all love interests have confessed their feelings and/or desire for something more. Before you shout "hooray" and start celebrating, remember this doesn't mean they are ready to rush off into the sunset on their white horses. You still need to write the sequel to this beat. That is where beat 7 comes to the rescue.

Beat 7—Reaction to confession

The possibility of a romantic relationship going forward is either accepted or rejected by those involved.

For this beat, you will need to:

- *Show your love interests reacting to the confession*

  This can be a positive, negative, or neutral reaction. The first one to confess might say they only want a one-night stand. The other love interest/s might agree to this, hoping it will resolve their feelings as well. Or they might ask for more time to decide, at which point they could seek wise counsel from a friend, parent, mentor, or sidekick.

Of course, there are other possible ways to react to a love confession, including an outright "no." Feel free to use your imagination. There is no right way, only the way that suits the characters and story.

To further elucidate: If the answer is "yes" or "maybe," you will need to write further scenes (and sequels) where the love interests spend more time together, receive deeper and more personal information about each other, and continue to get close. You make it seem like a future together is filled with love, hope, and infinite possibility (this is known as *false hope*). Then, the moment things are getting cozy, you will need to hint at trouble for their union. This is known as *foreshadowing the black moment* and should occur as close to the end of the third act as possible.

If the answer is "no", write further scenes showing the love interest who rejected the confession why they were wrong to do so, and wrong about the other person/s. They ultimately decide to embark on a relationship of some kind (even if they believe it's a casual or fling situation). The same is true for a "maybe" response.

Examples of the seventh beat in romance novels

From Beautiful

> Bella and Kit agree they want to see where a romantic relationship could lead them.

From Pride and Prejudice

> Unsurprisingly (to readers), Lizzie refuses Darcy's inept, rude, and arrogant proposal. She has no interest in pursuing anything romantic with him ... yet!

From Boyfriend Material

> Lucien and Oliver agree to continue as "not-so-fake-fake-boyfriends." This one is especially interesting because they both hang onto the "fake" title for a little longer.

Use these examples to draw out your own ideas in the following exercise.

Exercise 31. Beat 7—Reaction to confession

*You can refer to the notes you made for this beat during exercise 18 (Relationship arc).

How will your love interests react to the confession? Love interest 1_____

_____

_____

_____

Love interest 2_____

_____

_____

_____

Other love interests/further notes_____

_____

_____

Get your writing hands ready because it's time to write your seventh beat in your first draft. When that is complete, you can work through the other elements to consider before you can finish this act.

The *first kiss of commitment*

What I call the *first kiss of commitment* refers the first kiss the love interests have *after* the confession. It is termed this because the love interests could have kissed before this point, but it was not a committed kiss.

Beat 7 is the best time to place this kiss but it can happen any time after, or even at the time of the confession. You could also have an *almost first kiss of commitment* happen here, with the real one coming later, or a *rejected first kiss of commitment* anywhere before this point. The latter occurs when one of your love interests lunges at the other with a kiss that is stopped or pulled away from (Lucien does this to Oliver in *Boyfriend Material*). Even if these occur, both will need to turn into a real first kiss of commitment later on.

Exercise 32. The first kiss of commitment
Do you have a first kiss yet? If not, now is the time to let your mind wander with ways to incorporate this important aspect of a romance novel. Which type of kiss would suit

your story best (almost first kiss, rejected first kiss, or real first kiss)?_____

_____

_____

_____

_____

You know what to do. If you haven't, go and write your kissing scene in your first draft. If you have, is there a way to make it better? Once you've nailed the first kiss, you can think about the sexy scenes. I'm sure you already have thought about these scenes, but now you can get your hands, and not only your minds, dirty.

The *first lovemaking of commitment*

Depending on the romance subgenre you are writing in, you could add the *first lovemaking of commitment* in this act. Again, I call it this because the love interests could have had sexual contact before the desire for a commitment or relationship was voiced and agreed to.

This can also include an *almost first lovemaking of commitment*, where the lovers are interrupted before anything too sexual can take place.

Furthermore, the sex can occur on the page or off the page. The former means sex that is described in detail for the reader; the latter means you finish the sex scene when the bedroom (or car, elevator, office) door closes and leave it to the reader's imagination to fill in what happened.

Check your subgenre so you can follow the accepted conventions in this regard. For the most part, it's obvious. For instance, a Christian romance is going to be "clean" (no sex), whereas erotic romance is going to be a lot steamier. When you know what is and isn't accepted in your subgenre, start the below exercise.

Exercise 33. The first lovemaking of commitment
Do you have a first lovemaking scene yet? What level of sexual intimacy is accepted in your subgenre (clean, erotic, somewhere in between)? What type will it be (almost first lovemaking or real first lovemaking)?_____

_____

_____

_____

_____

This is the part where you get to have all the fun. If you've never written a sex scene before, there are plenty of blogs plus several books and workshops that can help you out. It's a skill just like writing (and sex); the more you practice, the better you will become. Either way, give it a go. This is only a first draft. First drafts are allowed to be bad and cheesy. You have my permission to write a terrible sex scene! You also have my permission to write the best sex of your life.

One more exercise, then you've finished the third act. Keep going.

How do I end the third act?

One of the main purposes of Act 3 is to ramp up the romance, action, feelings, and subplots. As the fourth act is called the *breakup*, you want to end the third act just before this seems likely to happen.

To do this successfully, you will need to show everything about to implode: Secrets are coming out, the truth is being uncovered, old enemies are closing in, or something happens that makes a character think a relationship now will be impossible. But one or more of the love interests don't know this yet ...

Exercise 34. Ending the third act.
Are there any secrets ready to come out? What ones? How will they come out?_____

_____

_____

_____

_____

Is the truth being uncovered? Who, what, when, where, why, and how?_____

_____

_____

_____

_____

Are any old enemies closing in? Who, what, when, where, and how?_____

_____

_____

_____

_____

Is something else happening that makes one or more love interest believe a relationship is impossible? What is it? Why does the love interest believe this? How will this ramp up, ready to explode in the fourth act?_____

_____

_____

_____

_____

What about a hook, teaser, or cliff hanger? Using your ideas above, is there a way you could create one?_____

_____

_____

_____

_____

Writing time. This is your final writing for act three, so make sure you give your third act ending some punch.

You are three-quarters of the way through your first draft. Pause and give yourself a pat on the back. Most aspiring writers don't make it this far, but YOU have!

Act 3 checklist

- o Is your beat six a confession of some kind? Do they admit it to themselves, a friend, or a love interest?

- o Does your seventh beat give a realistic reaction? Is the yes, no, or maybe response clear?

- o Have you followed up with the appropriate scenes and sequels to show the reaction?

- o Have you foreshadowed the impending black moment (the breakup) coming in Act 4 by having secrets or other information about to be revealed?

- o Did you sufficiently ramp up the romance, plots, and character development?

Chapter Seven

Act 4

How long should Act 4 be?

This is the next fifteen percent of the book.

The purpose of Act 4

I refer to the fourth act as the breakup because this is the section where the love interests are separated or break up in some way. It does not have to be a conventional argument and split, it can be an event that takes the couple away from each other (like a kidnapping). To hit the markers of this act, ensure you:

- o Make the obstacles so big that a relationship between the protagonist and love interest seems impossible, or is thwarted in some way

- o Break up (or separate) the love interests

- Make everything (a romance, external goals, anything else) seem doomed to failure.

How do I start the fourth act?

The fourth act starts with what is traditionally known as the *dark* or *black moment*. This is the part of the narrative when all seems lost. For romance, it is the break up of the relationship. It is the scene, or series of scenes, when everything the love interests thought they could build together seems unlikely, impossible, or strained. That is why you needed to end the third act in a way that prepared for this eventuality. Unlike the other acts, you can start the fourth act with its first beat, so let's look at the associated beats for this act in more detail.

How many beats make up the fourth act?

According to *The Romance Novel Formula,* there are two beats in the fourth act. They are the *rejection of relationship* and *misery.*

Beat 8—Rejection of relationship

Something happens that forces the couple apart (breaks them up). It can include something external, such as a kidnapping that physically removes the love interests from each other, or it can be an internal rejection, such as one or more of the love interests' fears/needs/flaws getting in the way. It can also be a misdirection, lie, reversal, or major misunderstanding. Remember, however, if you choose the latter, it cannot be something simple; nothing a quick conversation can resolve. If you do that, readers will feel cheated and not believe in the long-term success of the relationship.

For this beat, you will need to:

o *Break the lovers up!*

I think this point has been repeated enough, but have included examples below.

Examples of the eighth beat in romance novels

From Beautiful

> Kit is kidnapped. Hence, he and Bella are forced apart by external factors rather than internal reasons.

From Pride and Prejudice

> Lizzie's refusal of Darcy's marriage proposal breaks them up. Darcy tells her he will not repeat his offer to her, and they part on somewhat unfriendly terms, with both hoping they will never see the other again.

From Boyfriend Material

> During a disastrous time at Oliver's parents' anniversary party, and afraid of having shown himself to be "weak" and "never quite what someone is looking for," Oliver breaks up with Lucien.

Mull over these examples and see if you can think of an interesting breakup for your love interests to write below.

Exercise 35. Beat 8—Rejection of relationship.
*You can refer to the notes you made for this beat during exercise 18 (Relationship arc).
How can your love interests breakup? Do fears/needs/flaws interfere? Is it a misdirection, lie, reversal, or major misunderstanding? What about something external, like a kidnapping?_____

_____

_____

_____

_____

Does the catalyst for the breakup make a relationship seem unlikely, impossible, or strained? How?_____

_____

_____

_____

_____

Open your first draft and write the opening/beat 8 for your fourth act. Once the lovers are apart, you can show them dwelling in their own version of misery.

Beat 9—Misery

The love interests are miserable being apart. This can be shown through mourning their loss of each other, missing each other, longing for each other, or thinking about each other.

There can be an attempt to move on from the breakup. Characters can do this by jumping into the new life they created by being involved with the love interest/s, or by reverting to old patterns of behavior (or looking like they will) as a way to cope with the misery.

For this beat, you will need to:

o *Show* all *the lovers stuck in misery.*

Write reactions to the breakup/separation for all of the involved love interests, even if it is one sentence long. You *can* have the focus on one character, but your manuscript will be stronger if you incorporate the responses of all love interests. A reminder not to tell us they are missing each other, but instead show us in their thoughts, their actions, and the way they are going about their lives. Again, the possibilities here are endless.

Examples of the nineth beat in romance novels

From Beautiful

> Bella finds it near-impossible to concentrate and function while the search for Kit carries on. Kit almost reverts to his former self while he is being held captive.

From Pride and Prejudice

> Lizzie learns the truth about Mr. Wickham. On a sightseeing visit to Darcy's home, Pemberley, the housekeeper informs them of the wonderful side to Darcy's nature. Lizzie starts to regret refusing Darcy's offer. After her sister, Lydia, causes a scandal that could ruin the family, Lizzie fears she has lost her chance with Darcy completely. Darcy has already concluded that he has lost Lizzie, and deals with this by improving

his behavior (*this* is why women swoon for Mr. Darcy).

From Boyfriend Material

Lucien talks about how the breakup ruined his "Sunday, Monday, Tuesday, and possibly my life" and how he "feels useless and heartbroken."

These three stories deal with the misery beat in different ways. It is your turn to brainstorm some misery scenes.

Exercise 36. Beat 9—Misery.
*You can refer to the notes you made for this beat during exercise 18 (Relationship arc).
How can your love interests suffer? Is it interesting and unique (as well as relevant to the story)? Love interest 1___

_____

_____

_____

_____

Love interest 2_____

_____

_____

_____

_____

Other love interests/further notes_____

_____

_____

     Turn these notes into a heart-wrenching beat in your first draft. There are no extra points to keep in mind for the fourth act. You can move straight to the ending.

How do I end the fourth act?

End the fourth act with a hook that will make the reader want to see how the separation or breakup will be resolved (they are reading romance, so they know it will be resolved. Don't try to be too clever here or it will annoy readers). The hook can be a thought, question, or action that hints at the way the relationship will be saved and how the love interests will *make up* in Act 5.

Exercise 37. Ending the fourth act.

What thought, question, or action can you use to hint at the
way the relationship will be saved?_____

_____

_____

_____

_____

Write the chosen ending into your first draft. **That is
one more act finished. You are on the home stretch now!**

Act 4 checklist

- o   Have you shown a believable and sufficient
  rejection or separation (beat 8) for the breakup
  scene?

- o   Have you shown believable and relevant misery
  (beat 9) scene?

- o   Do they feel realistic and believable to the story you
  are telling?

- o   Have you started the fourth act with the black
  moment that paves the way for the breakup?

o   Have you ended the fourth act with a hook hinting at

the makeup to come in Act 5?

Chapter Eight

Act 5

How long should Act 5 be?

Act 5 encompasses the final ten percent of the book.

The purpose of Act 5

I refer to the final act as the *makeup* because the love interest and protagonist find their way back to each other. Therefore, the main purposes of this act are:

- To reunite the love interests (get them to make up)
- To wrap up all main and subplots
- To make a relationship between the love interests seem like it will be solid and lasting
- To create a satisfactory happily-ever-after (H.E.A.) or happy-for-now (H.F.N.).

How do I start the fifth act?

The fifth act should start with a scene or scenes that work to get the love interests back together. Like the fourth act, you can start the final act by writing the first beat.

How many beats make up the fifth act?

According to *The Romance Novel Formula,* there are two beats in the final act. They are the *come together* and *H.E.A.* or *H.F.N.*

Beat 10—Come together

Something happens, or someone makes a decision/changes their mind, that brings the love interests back together. They are reunited and dedicated to each other and a proper, committed relationship.

For this beat, you will need to:

- o *Show the reunion*

    This can be one brief scene or several larger scenes that reunite the lovers. It can be a comedy of errors, a set-up by their friends, a coincidence, a glimpse of one love interest doing something admirable that changes the other's mind. Pick whatever suits the story and characters best. Also, if one of the characters has stuffed up in a major way, there will need to be some sort of grand gesture, grovel, or sacrifice made on their part in order to deserve the happiness and relationship. If the makeup is not aligned in correct proportion to the breakup, it will put readers off.

Examples of the tenth beat in romance novels

From *Beautiful*

Bella is kidnapped and brought to the same place Kit is being held. They are reunited, but imprisoned. However, they find a way to escape.

From *Pride and Prejudice*

After standing up to Darcy's aunt, who rudely arrives unannounced at the Bennet home and starts to berate Lizzie, Darcy shows up. He repeats his offer of marriage.

From *Boyfriend Material*

Lucien tracks down Oliver and tries to get him to see how good they are together, but Oliver still refuses … until several hours later, when Oliver shows up at Lucien's doorstep and pleads for another chance.

Exercise 38. Beat 10—Come together.
*You can refer to the notes you made for this beat during exercise 18 (Relationship arc).

How can your love interests reunite? Is it a comedy of errors, a set-up by their friends, a coincidence, a glimpse of one love interest doing something admirable, or something else?____

_____

_____

_____

_____

_____

Go to your first draft and use these notes to write the come together scene. Naturally, the reunion leads to part of the novel that the reader (and love interests) has been waiting for all along.

Beat 11—H.E.A. or H.F.N.

This beat shows the love interests living happily-ever-after (H.E.A.) or happy-for-now (H.F.N.). Sometimes, this takes place in the form of an epilogue, but it can also be the closing chapter. Again, whichever works for your story and characters is best. Use this beat to end the story on a happy, positive, and satisfactory note. If there is no H.E.A. or H.F.N, it is not a romance novel. Make it as upbeat as you can.

For this beat, you will need to:

- *Have a second confession*

  This is the scene where all love interests admit/know they love each other and belong together. As such, they profess their love and commitment.

- o *Show the happy*

  Show the reader how happy and right the love interests are together.

- o *Wrap it up.*

  If you have not already, now is the time to ensure all subplots and main plots are wrapped up. Of course, you need to be wrapping up sections of your story throughout, but now is the time to double check you haven't left any questions unanswered or threads untied.

Examples of the final beat in romance novels

From *Beautiful*

Bella and Kit affirm their love for each other and decide they want to be together despite their differences.

From *Pride and Prejudice*

> Darcy asks Lizzie if her feelings for him are the same as they were when he'd proposed. She admits they have changed and she is now in love with him. He proposes again. Lizzie accepts, and they are married. According to Jane Austen, they live happily ever after—and who are we to question her!

From *Boyfriend Material*

> Lucien and Oliver admit the feelings they have for each other are real. Oliver asks if they should try again. Lucien agrees, saying, "Let's be terrified together."

Three books. Three examples of how wonderful, different, and utterly satisfying a romance novel ending can feel. The emphasis on that last sentence should be the word *satisfying*. You want readers to feel happy by the end of your book … because that is why they bought it.

Exercise 39. Beat 11—H.E.A. or H.F.N.

*You can refer to the notes you made for this beat during exercise 18 (Relationship arc).

What will your second confession entail?_____

_____

_____

_____

_____

_____

How will you show the happy?_____

_____

_____

_____

_____

_____

_____

What subplots need to be wrapped up?_____

_____

_____

_____

_____

Get your first draft, and yourself, ready and write up the final beat.

How do I end the fifth act?

You've done it already. **Yes, that means you have officially completed the first draft of your breakout romance novel! Write "The end" and smile. I hope you feel as proud of yourself as I am of you.**

Act 5 checklist

- o Have you reunited your love interests in a believable way? Is there a sufficient grand gesture, grovel, or sacrifice?

- o Can your final beat be classed as a H.E.A. or H.F.N?

- o Is your ending satisfying, positive, and happy?

- o Are all main plots and subplots concluded and wrapped up?

Now that you have reached the end of your story,

what's next?

Chapter Nine

What now?

If you are a plotter, you would have been able to outline and write your first draft using this guide. Your next step is to write a second draft, focusing on making each section tighter and stronger. With each subsequent draft, come back to *The Romance Novel Formula* and read over the acts and beats to ensure you have everything a successful romance novel needs.

If you are a pantser, you can wait until you have a workable draft before using the notes you made in exercise 18, or you can use each section of this guide as you work. Either way, once you have finished your first draft, it is probably a good idea to go through *The Romance Novel Formula* to make sure you have hit all the required markers. If you haven't, then you know where you need to turn your attention.

For all you plantsers, use a little of both approaches until you find the combination that works for you.

Once you are happy with your manuscript, you can work on your proposed blurb and synopsis. Whether you plan to publish independently, traditionally, or hybrid (a combination of the two), these will need to be written. Some writers prefer to work on these *before* they start their outline and others like to write them after their first draft. Whichever method you choose, blurbs and synopses are outside the purpose of this book. However, there are plenty of blogs, websites, online courses, and books you can check out.

That's all, my "loveleigh" romance writers

Even though you have reached the end of this guidebook, I have my fingers crossed that this is the beginning of your romance writing career. I will not tell you that the path is easy, only that it is rewarding in more ways than you know. The lovers' journey is not limited to the one your characters will take. With each book you write, you will learn more about yourself, your writing, and, most importantly, love.

Yours in love, writing, and romance books,

Alicia Leigh

www.fallinlovewithleigh.com

*

Thank you for reading *THE ROMANCE NOVEL FORMULA*! Remember that positive reviews help the author. If you enjoyed this book, please consider marking it 5-stars on Amazon or Goodreads. With much appreciation, Alicia Leigh xo

*

You can find out more about me and join my LOVELEIGHS CLUB for exclusive competitions and giveaways, special offers, author news, free excerpts, and more via my website: www.fallinlovewithleigh.com

Suggested Reading and Websites

Books
1.   Alderson, M 2011, *The Plot Whisperer: Secrets of Story Structure Any Writer Can Master*, Adams Media, U.S.A.
2.   Booker, C 2006, *The Seven Basic Plots: Why We Tell Stories*, Bloomsbury, London.
3.   Brody, J 2018, *Save The Cat! Writes a Novel: The Last Book on Novel Writing You'll Ever Need*, Ten Speed Press, U.S.A.
4.   Brooks, L 2011, *Story Engineering: Mastering the 6 Core Competencies of Successful Writing*, Writer's Digest Books, U.S.A.
5.   Campbell, J 1949, *The Hero with a Thousand Faces*, Harper Collins, London.
6.   Cron, L 2016, *Story Genius: How to Use Brain Science to Go Beyond Outlining and Write a Riveting Novel,* Ten Speed Press, U.S.A.
7.   Hague, M. 2011 (2nd ed.), *Writing Screenplays that Sell: The Complete Guide to Turning Story Concepts into Movie and Television Deals,* Collins Reference, U.K.
8.   Hayes, G. 2016, *Romancing the Beat: Story Structure for Romance Novels*, Gwen Hayes, U.S.A.
9.   McKee, R 1998, *Story*, Methuen, London.
10.   McIntosh, F 2015, *How to Write Your Blockbuster: All I've Learned About Writing Commercial Fiction,* Penguin Books, Australia.
11.   Sykes, C 2013, *How to Craft a Great Story,* Hodder & Stoughton, London.
12.   Vogler, C 1992, *The Writer's Journey: Mythic Structure for Storytellers and Screenwriters*, Michael Wise Productions, California.
13.   Yorke, J 2013, *Into the Woods,* Penguin Random House, U.K.

Websites
1.   Martha Alderson www.marthaalderson.com/

2.   Jessica Brody www.jessicabrody.com/
3.   Laurel Cohn www.laurelcohn.com.au/
4.   Lisa Cron www.wiredforstory.com/
5.   Entangled Publishing
www.entangledpublishing.com
6.   Michael Hague www.storymastery.com/
8.   Harlequin Mills & Boon
     www.harlequin.com/shop/index and
     www.millsandboon.co.uk/
9.   Fiona McIntosh www.fionamcintosh.com/
10. Chris Sykes www.chrissykes.uk/
11. Christopher Vogler
www.chrisvogler.wordpress.com/
12. John Yorke www.johnyorkestory.com/

Appendix A: Preliminaries worksheet

Exercise 1. What romance readers want from their fiction

Which *reader wants* does your manuscript offer? Circle those that might apply:

Entertainment   Escape   Relaxation

Further notes_____

_____

_____

Exercise 2. Theme

What main theme could *express your ideas about life and/or human nature*? Write several possibilities below.

_____

_____

_____

_____

Further notes_____

_____

_____

Exercise 3. Tone/Mood/Atmosphere

List some ways that you add a unique *tone* (approach) to your work:

_____

_____

_____

_____

What overall *mood* (feelings) are you looking to convey?

_____

_____

_____

_____

_____

What *atmosphere* (reader experience) are you hoping to create for the reader?

_____

_____

_____

_____

_____

Further notes_____

_____

_____

Exercise 4. Setting/Place/Time
What setting, year, season, weather, places, and times do you need to keep track of in your novel? List them below.

_____

_____

_____

_____

_____

Exercise 5. Tropes
List 1–3 relevant tropes that would suit your novel.

_____

_____

_____

_____

_____

Do you have a "writerly trope?" List it below.

_____

_____

Exercise 6. Master plots
Jot at least one relevant master plot here.

_____
_____
_____
_____
_____

Exercise 7. Archetypes

Which of the twelve common archetypes suit your main
love interests? Write them below.

_____
_____
_____
_____
_____

Exercise 8. Where's the bond?

How do you show the five romantic relationship bonds in
your story? List them, or ways you can show them.

Physical_____
_____
_____
_____
_____

Emotional_____
_____
_____
_____
_____

Mental_____
_____
_____
_____
_____

Sexual_____
_____
_____
_____
_____

Spiritual_____

_____

_____

_____

_____

Further notes_____

_____

_____

Exercise 9. The five characters every novel should have.

List your five main characters.

Love interest (love interest 1)_____

Love interest 2 (and others)_____

Sidekick/best friend forever_____

Mentor_____

Antagonist_____

Further notes_____

_____

_____

Exercise 10. Writing mistakes I need to look out for.

Show versus Tell_____

Active voice_____

Lapses in point of view_____

Weak voice_____

Clichés_____

Similar sentence length throughout_____

Lack of sense/s_____

Adverbs_____

Very and Just (filler, filter, crutch words)_____

Thinking punctuation isn't important_____

Formatting_____

Further notes_____

_____

_____

Appendix B: G.M.C. Worksheet

Love Interest 1	Love Interest 2
Goal: What does the character want?	Goal: What does the character want?
Motivation: Why does the character want it?	Motivation: Why does the character want it?
Conflict: Why can't the character get what they want?	Conflict: Why can't the character get what they want?

What are the relationship conflicts keeping the love interests apart?

_____

_____

_____

Appendix C: F.N.F Worksheet

Love Interest 1	Love Interest 2
Fear: What does the character fear? What is their wound?	**Fear: What does the character fear? What is their wound?**
Need: What does the character really need?	**Need: What does the character really need?**
Flaw: Why can't they resolve the fear and admit their true need?	**Flaw: Why can't they resolve the fear and admit their true need?**

Other notes?

_____

_____

_____

_____

Appendix D: *The Romance Novel Formula* Beat Sheet Template

ACT 1: The Setup (0-25%, first quarter of the book)
1. Introduction of the first love interest (LI1)
2. First interaction.
3. Something forces them together.

ACT 2: The Hookup (25-50%, next quarter of the book)
4. Denial of, or misguided, feelings.
5. Feelings get harder to deny.

ACT 3: The Ramp-up (50-75%, next quarter of the book)
6. Confession of feelings.
7. Reaction to confession.

ACT 4: The Breakup (75-90%, next 15% of the book)
8. Rejection of relationship.
9. Misery.

ACT 5: The Makeup (90-100%, final 10% of the book)
10. Come together.
11. H.E.A. or H.F.N.